the mothercare guide to
BABY CLOTHES
— AND —
EQUIPMENT

Heather Welford

Conran Octopus

Project editor	Jane O'Shea
Editor	Emma Russell
Project assistant	Debora Robertson
Art editor	Alison Shackleton
Production	Shane Lask
Illustrations	Lucy Su
	Linda Worrall
Jacket photograph	Andy Cox

First published in 1989 by
Conran Octopus Limited
37 Shelton Street
London WC2H 9HN

Copyright © 1989 Conran Octopus

Reprinted 1989

ISBN 1 85029 141 1

Typeset by Bookworm Typesetting, Manchester
Printed by Eagle Press plc, Scotland

CONTENTS

Introduction **4**

First clothes **6**

Feedtime **14**

Nappies and nappy changing **22**

Bathtime **30**

Bedtime **36**

Your day with your baby **42**

Out and about **48**

Safety around the house **58**

Useful addresses **62**

Index **63**

INTRODUCTION

Congratulations! Whether you're expecting a baby or you've just become proud new parents, you're at the start of an exciting time. You'll experience many changes over the next twenty years and right from the start you'll be faced with lots of decisions to do with your baby's needs. It can seem quite daunting at first, wondering how many stretchsuits will be needed in the early weeks and deciding which type of plastic pants to choose, let alone weighing up the different advantages offered by the vast choice of baby transport.

The aim of this book is to make some of these decisions that much easier. There is such a vast array of baby goods available these days that it can be very difficult to decide what will be useful to you and your family – and what will turn out to be one of those bad buys that never get used. After all, you probably won't have taken much notice of what is available for babies until now – and here you are, faced with the need to equip, clothe and cater for your very own.

The most important part of parenting is not to do with the sort of clothes your baby wears, or what type of baby transport you buy, or the design of highchair you settle on. The love that grows between you and your baby and the pride you'll have in watching him develop into a happy, healthy, confident little person is what really counts. But your love for and pride in your baby can develop best if you are confident about all aspects of caring for him. This book will take some of the small headaches away and answer some of your questions about the practical side of looking after a baby. And that will allow you to get on with what you are best at: being a mum or dad!

Whether you decide to buy new or second-hand goods for your baby, there are certain important factors, apart from the obvious one of cost, that you should bear in mind. Clothes should fit well, but not too tightly, particularly at your baby's neck, wrists and feet. Check that furniture and toys are well-made and sturdy, with no sharp points or edges and no awkward angles where tiny fingers could become trapped. Materials used in their construction should be safe and non-toxic. When choosing wheeled transport for your new baby, make sure that the brakes are firm and effective and that any folding mechanism on a stroller or pushchair has a primary and secondary device to prevent it folding up when your child is sitting in it. Carrycots, prams, pushchairs and highchairs should be fitted with 'D' rings for the attachment of a separate safety harness (unless the item has its own integral five-point harness).

The British Standards Institution produces strict safety standards for the manufacture of a wide range of nursery equipment and toys, so if you are buying new, check whether the item meets the BS requirements. Some goods may carry the BSI kitemark or number on a label or swing ticket, but if you can't see one, ask – assistants in any reputable store or shop should know if their merchandise complies with the safety requirements. If you buy or are given second-hand items, you won't have the consumer protection that you have when buying new, but you should still check that the goods comply with the safety standards.

Having this book with you, whether you're buying new, second-hand or a mixture of both, will give you sensible guidelines on the range of items available from the very start of your baby's life. As well as information on clothes and equipment, there are useful tips on feeding, nappy changing, bathing and dressing. There are a number of ideas to help you when you're fixing up a room for your baby, plus tips on entertaining your baby and on making his environment as safe as possible. I hope that they will all help you to enjoy your baby and the new life that lies ahead of you!

This book is one of a series of Mothercare Guides that covers topics of immediate interest to parents of young children. The books are all fully illustrated and offer clear and straightforward guidance on practical aspects of everyday childcare. The other titles available in the series are listed on the back jacket of this book.

All the information in these books applies equally to male and female children. To reflect this, the pronouns 'he' and 'she' have been used in alternating chapters throughout each book. Where, occasionally, the text does apply to a particular sex, the appropriate pronoun is used.

FIRST CLOTHES

Choosing clothes for your new baby can be one of the nicest parts of pregnancy and early parenthood. The choice of baby clothes available today is wider than ever before and it's fun to look through all that is on offer. However, it can all be rather bewildering as well if you aren't prepared with information on what garments the baby will need, how they are sized, and on practical considerations such as how easy they are to wash and how many you'll need.

WHERE TO BUY

Chain stores like Mothercare offer excellent value for money and a superb 'head-to-toe' collection of everything you need. Baby sections in the larger department stores may give you a wider choice of brand-names and price range. Upmarket baby boutiques are best for special occasion outfits only, unless money really is no object with your family! At the other end of the scale, you can sometimes pick up good bargains in small, independent haberdashery shops. However, the most consistently good value comes from trusted brands or own-brand merchandise.

WEAR AND TEAR

Baby garments do need to be hard-wearing – not because your baby is going to give her clothing rough treatment, but because you will be washing them such a lot, and fastening and unfastening them frequently because of nappy changing. Poorly-made baby clothes – and that does not necessarily mean the cheapest – in impractical fabrics look tired and shapeless after a few washes and start to weaken very quickly at their fastening points.

It will be easier for you if most of your baby's clothes can be machine-washed. Hand-washing a few garments won't be too arduous, of course, but as you can probably count on receiving a few delicate 'hand-wash only' knits as presents, it's a good idea to check that the items you buy yourself are machine-washable.

CHOOSING FABRICS AND COLOURS

Natural fibres are comfortable next to the skin and pure cotton is the best choice for underwear for your new baby. It is a matter of preference whether you choose only natural fibres for the rest of your baby's clothing. Man-made fabrics, or mixtures of natural and man-made, have much improved in terms of 'feel' and they wash and dry very well. A few babies appear to develop a sensitivity to certain artificial fibres, however, and if this happens to your baby you will be pleased with the choice of pure cotton garments available today.

It will help you to cut down your ironing load if you choose fabrics such as velour, towelling, sweatshirt material and knitted fabrics.

Traditionally, babies are dressed in white, with pink as an option for a girl and pale blue for a boy. Don't let tradition narrow your choice, though, if you don't want it to! Babies' clothes now come in all colours of the rainbow, and though putting a baby in orange or deep turquoise still sounds unusual, with the right styling and fabric these colours can look just right. If you don't want to go for the newer, brighter colours, or if you just want to ring the changes, other pastels are always an alternative: try pale lilac, soft jade or primrose yellow.

UNDERSTANDING SIZING

There is no standard way that baby clothes are sized and one manufacturer's so-called first size may be a lot smaller than another's. Babies come in different lengths and shapes as well, so a lot of your selection has to be made on intelligent guesswork. As a general rule, there is little point in getting many items in the very smallest sizes, as these are the sort of clothes that friends and relatives are likely to give you as presents. In addition, babies grow out of these tiny garments very quickly indeed – long before you feel they have had sufficient wear – and whereas it is easy to put a largish garment on a young baby, you should not squeeze chubby arms and legs into something that is too small or tight.

Some manufacturers base their sizing on length, generally starting at fifty-five centimetres (twenty-two inches) which fits a baby from birth to about two months. The sizes then increase at five or ten centimetre (two or four inch) intervals. Other manufacturers still use chest measurements to size their garments. As a rule, the smallest size is forty centimetres (sixteen inches) and the sizings go up in intervals of five centimetres (two inches). A fifty-centimetre (twenty-inch) chest will fit a baby of about a year old. Another way that you might find clothes sized is by age, such as zero to three months.

EASY DRESSING

Do look at the way the clothes you choose are actually designed and take into account the ease with which you will be able to dress and undress your baby. The very best and most practical garments from this point of view are the ones that allow you easy access to the nappy for changing. This means, for example, stretchsuits are best if they have poppers or zippers down the inside of each leg as a crotch opening. Some trousers and pull-on dungarees have this sort of design as well. An extra-long zip fastening that goes down at least one leg is a useful feature on outer clothing, like snowsuits.

Clothes which fasten down the front are a lot easier to put on and take off than back-fastening ones. A tiny baby may not like being turned backwards and forwards simply so you can get her dressed, and if everything fastens coat-style you will disturb her far less. This is why many parents prefer first vests that fasten with ties at the front, rather than the ones which pull on over the head. However, an envelope-style neck on a vest means it can be pulled on over the head with minimum fuss.

WHAT YOUR NEWBORN WILL NEED

Our very basic list of all the clothing you need for your new baby is no more than a guide – you may have different preferences and priorities – but it can be reassuring to know that if you follow it you are unlikely to run short of anything really important (for details of nappies and waterproof pants, see pages 22–26). You will need:

> ► vests and/or bodysuits: at least four
> ► all-in-one stretchsuits and/or other outfits: at least six
> ► cardigans/matinée jackets: at least two
> ► hats: two
> ► bootees/socks: one or two pairs
> ► mittens: one or two pairs
> ► shawls: one or two.

If washing and drying baby clothes is likely to be difficult for you – for instance, if you don't have a washing machine or a place outside to dry washing in the absence of a tumble drier – you will need more than the basics above. It may sound a lot for an essential wardrobe, but you really will need plenty of clean clothes in reserve at all times! Babies often bring up a little milk after a feed, for example, and even the best-fitting nappy leaks at times, so when that happens you may need to change your baby from the skin up – maybe as often as twice a day or more.

If you use a stretchsuit (which covers the feet) as your baby's basic day and night attire, you won't need more than one pair of socks or bootees for her to wear when it's very cold. Similarly, mittens won't be

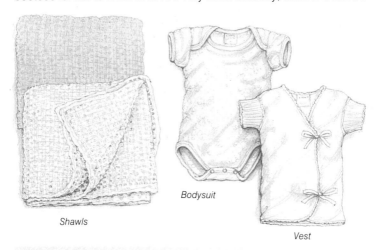

Shawls

Bodysuit

Vest

TIPS

▶ Remember that your baby's skin is delicate, so check the inside of clothes for rough seams that could chafe her.

▶ If knitting friends or relatives offer to make something for your baby, it might be a good idea to encourage them to knit items such as cardigans instead of bootees or mittens which are cheap to buy ready-made.

Mittens

Bootees

► *See pages 22–26 for nappies*

worn very often if you have stretchsuits or other outfits with turn-back mitten cuffs to keep her hands warm.

Hats are essential in winter and even a summer baby needs one or two, though during a hot summer you should use a cotton sun bonnet instead. A baby who is well wrapped up in a cardigan or jacket and shawl and tucked in under sufficient pram bedding does not need an outdoor garment (though see Useful extras, page 10) as she will be cosy enough, even in cold weather. Small babies don't toss and turn and wriggle out of their blankets. If the shawl you choose is not too bulky, you can simply double it and wrap a winter baby in it – or leave it single thickness for a summer baby.

You will need cardigans or matinée jackets – these are cardigans which fasten at the top only and then flare out at the bottom to make room for a nappy – whatever time of year your baby is born. A jumper is an alternative, but do check the neck-opening is wide enough. An envelope-style neckline or one with a button-opening on one shoulder is best.

Unless you feel strongly about it, you do not really need to worry about different styling for boys and girls these days, although some parents still like, for example, to put a boy in a helmet-style hat and a girl in a bonnet. If you stick to basic styling when buying your newborn's clothes, you will find you can buy all you need in advance of the birth and feel very organized!

SAFETY

▶ Lacy knits look delightful, but if the design is very loose or 'holey', little fingers can get caught, causing discomfort and irritation.
▶ Make sure that socks, bootees and the feet of all-in-one garments (like tights and stretchsuits) allow enough growing room for toes – too tight garments can damage your baby's feet.

Hat

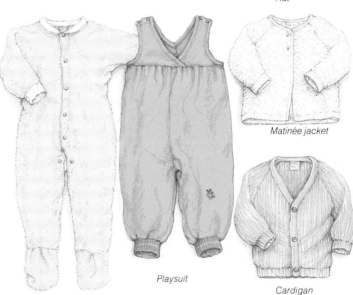

Matinée jacket

Playsuit

Cardigan

Stretchsuit

A SUMMER BABY – OR A WINTER ONE?

Our essentials list will be fine for a new baby born at whatever time of the year. You can simply adjust your baby's layers according to the temperature, removing or adding a shawl or cardigan.

In extremely hot weather, your baby will be fine in a nappy and vest or tee-shirt with a sun hat, though never leave her directly in the sun.

When it comes to choosing extras, you will find the choice in the shops reflects the different seasons. In the spring and summer, you might like to pick one or two items with short sleeves or short legs, but remember always to use a sunscreen on your baby's exposed skin. For girls, you will find pretty dresses, and for boys, lightweight rompers. In winter, you can choose chunkier jumpers or sweatshirts and maybe a pramsuit or knitted jacket and leggings.

USEFUL EXTRAS

Our list of baby's essentials will get you through the first few months, but there are other garments that could prove useful to you as well or that you might choose simply because you like them.

▶ Scratch mittens – tiny mitts to wear indoors, usually made of soft cotton. They will protect your baby from scratching her face.

▶ Bibs – if your baby wears a bib, you will avoid some of the clothes-changing that may be necessary with a dribbly baby.

▶ Coloured vest or tee-shirt – this will look more attractive than an ordinary vest on hot summer days when you need to dress your baby in only the bare minimum.

▶ Fabric briefs – worn over waterproof pants or an all-in-one disposable, these will help to hold the nappy in place and give a smoother 'line' under clothing. They look smarter under dresses, too.

▶ Baby gowns – these can make nappy changing much easier, especially at night when you don't want to disturb your baby too much. They may not be very practical for an older, wriggly baby unless you choose ones with a closure at the hem to stop them riding up.

▶ Sleeping bag/pramsuit – these garments normally have a hood and they are an alternative to putting your baby in a shawl and hat when going outdoors.

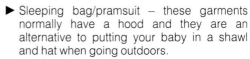

SAFETY

▶ Choose garments without drawstrings or ribbons round wrists, ankles or neck.

DRESSING YOUR BABY

Make sure that you are in a warm room with no draughts when you are dressing your baby and that you have everything you need at hand. Put your baby on a changing mat or on a towel or sheet. It doesn't matter whether you place this on the floor, on the bed, changing unit or table, or if your baby is in her cot or crib (though you will only be able to use a table, bed or changing unit while she is very small and unable to roll over). In any case, you should always stay near your baby when she is on a raised surface as a sudden movement or unexpected roll could cause her to fall. You might prefer to dress your baby while holding her on your lap and, in fact, some babies seem to like this better. It is up to you to find out what you can do most easily and what suits you and your baby best.

HOW TO DRESS YOUR BABY

1. Put on your baby's nappy first and waterproof pants if she wears them. Then you can put on her vest or bodysuit. If it has an envelope neck, stretch the neck wide before you put it on. Slip it over your baby's head, supporting the back of her head as you do so.

2. Holding one sleeve open, take your baby's hand and guide it gently through the sleeve. Do the same with the other sleeve and carefully pull the vest down.

3. Put on front-fastening garments, like stretchsuits, as if they were a jacket, that is, arms in the sleeves first. Gather up one sleeve in your hand, slip this over the baby's wrists and unroll the sleeve up her arm. Do the same with the other sleeve.

4. Next, guide one of your baby's legs in, then the other, and fasten up the stretchsuit. You can then put on any outer garments you wish.

CLOTHES FOR YOUR OLDER BABY

At about the age of three or four months, and often earlier with 'fast-growing' babies, you will find you need larger clothes for your child. You may need to change her clothes slightly less frequently than you did before, however, as she won't be quite so 'sicky' or so abundant with her bowel and bladder productions! At the same time, you will both have developed more of a predictable routine and you will be able to make a distinction between what your baby wears in the day and what she wears at night, and this will probably mean you actually need more items of clothing than before.

Your baby's growth slows down after the age of three months or so, so the clothes you buy now will last a little longer before they become too small. Stretchsuits are still about the most practical basic garment you can buy and you may find you continue to have at least a couple in use right up to the time your baby starts walking.

You will still need a minimum of six vests, six outfits for daytime and three or four jumpers or cardigans for your baby as she grows. Other clothing bought for the newborn period – hats, shawls, mittens – will probably still fit, but bootees and socks will need changing regularly to allow for growth.

NIGHTWEAR

In addition to the above, you will need a minimum of three night-time garments. Previously, you will not have found it necessary to change your baby every evening simply because she was going to bed for the night – and most parents find that they make no real distinction between night and day wear during the very early months. This will probably change once your baby is being bathed every evening and you are into more of a routine.

You can find a delightful choice of baby pyjamas or nighties, or stretchsuits with moon and star designs, if you want. On the other hand, your baby will not mind a bit if her night-time attire consists of second-hand garments that you have had passed on to you!

A cosy garment that is ideal for soon-to-be-toddlers is a walk-in sleeper. Worn over pyjamas, this all-in-one, zip-up coverall keeps your baby warm no matter how much she roughs up her covers.

OUT OF DOORS

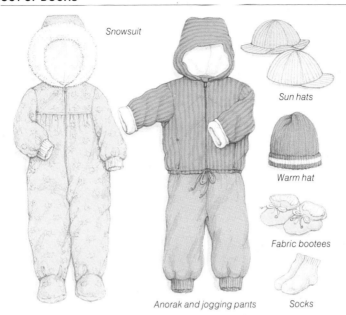

Snowsuit

Sun hats

Warm hat

Fabric bootees

Anorak and jogging pants   Socks

Older babies need outer garments more than younger ones do. Covers get wriggled out of, for a start, and babies who until now have been in a pram, or carrycot and transporter, are likely to have at least occasional outings in a pushchair or stroller where they will need more protection from the cold. For cooler days in high summer, a jacket or anorak on top of a cardigan, if necessary, may be all you need. At other times, your baby will need a zip-in snowsuit or coat, or jacket and warm leggings. Check that a zip-in snowsuit is fitted with a long zip to make it easier to put on and take off. If you can wash and dry things quickly, you probably only need one outfit like this. Otherwise, buy two.

Except on very warm days, your baby will need socks, knitted bootees or pull-on fabric bootees. These can also be worn over stretchsuits or other garments with feet, on the days when you feel something extra is needed to keep little toes from getting cold.

Don't forget that a hat is still essential on cold days, and a sun hat is needed in high summer to prevent your baby's scalp and neck getting burnt. If she really *won't* wear one, you will definitely need to use a parasol (see page 55).

CLOTHING FOR BABIES ON THE MOVE

Once your baby can crawl — this may be at any time from around seven months — and becomes more mobile generally, nighties, if you've used them at all, are impractical. Little girls' dresses are uncomfortable for crawlers, too — the hem gets caught on the feet and the knees! You can now find a much better selection of girl-style rompers for this awkward stage.

Pull-on trousers or playsuits are very practical for this age group. Jogging suits in sweatshirt fabric always look smart and fashionable, and are quick to wash and dry (and need no ironing). Buy two in co-ordinating colours for a mix-and-match look.

FEEDTIME

For the first few months, you will be breastfeeding or bottlefeeding your baby. This provides all the nourishment he needs in the initial months until his digestive system is mature enough to cope with solids (foods other than milk).

There are no hard and fast rules about what your baby should eat and drink, and when. Be guided by his progress and development, and take advice from your health visitor who will help you work out what is best of you and your baby. Some babies seem ready for solids sooner than others and some babies are happiest taking the whole business of weaning from a milk-only diet very slowly and gradually. Speaking very generally, though, the pattern most often recommended as suiting the majority of babies looks like this:

MONTHS ONE TO FOUR
Milk only, breast or baby formula.
To buy: bottlefeeding equipment (see page 16); breastfeeding accessories (see opposite); bibs (see page 10).

MONTHS FIVE TO SIX
Very gradual introduction of solids, in addition to milk (breast or baby formula), to accustom your baby to new tastes and textures. You can try him with a spouted cup for some drinks, but most babies don't learn to cope with this until much later.
To buy: bowls, spoons, cups (see pages 19–20).

MONTHS SEVEN TO EIGHT
Greater variety of solids, in increasing quantities, so he has three separate meals a day in addition to milk (breast or baby formula).
To buy: highchair (see page 21).

MONTHS NINE TO TWELVE
By the end of this time, your baby may be eating the same foods as the rest of the family (though his portion must be well chopped or mashed with no salt added). Milk can be either breast, baby formula or whole pasteurized ('silver top'). ·
To buy: a foldaway table seat (see page 21) if needed.

BREAST OR BOTTLE?

The major decision you will make when it comes to feeding your baby is whether to breastfeed or bottlefeed. Breastfeeding is undoubtedly better for your child's health and it gives first-class nutrition that is ideally suited to your baby's digestion. Antibodies in breast milk protect against illness and infection, and it is also important in helping to prevent allergies, such as eczema and asthma.

When breastfeeding goes well, it is a very satisfying experience for both you and your baby, so if you find you have problems with it – and many women do, especially at first – don't give up the whole idea! Instead, ask your midwife, health visitor or breastfeeding counsellor (see page 62 for address) for advice. With the right information, most breastfeeding problems are very short-lived.

Although most women begin by breastfeeding, some decide right from the start that it is not for them. Others make the switch from breast to bottle because they have not had the right sort of help with problems, and breastfeeding just is not working well for them. It is important to feel happy with your method of feeding and you shouldn't feel guilty if you decide that you would rather bottlefeed. Disappointment and regret are natural, though, if you had planned to breastfeed – but it will help to remember that if bottlefeeding is done correctly, a bottlefed baby is likely to thrive.

WEANING

Weaning – the gradual introduction of foods other than milk – should not begin too soon and between four and six months is generally thought to be right for most babies. Before six months, your main aim is to get your baby used to a few different tastes and textures, rather than to replace much of the milk in his diet. Milk should form the main part of your baby's intake for most of his first year, so there is no need to force the pace.

WHAT YOU NEED FOR BREASTFEEDING

Although some women breastfeed without buying anything special at all, there are several useful items which can make breastfeeding easier and more comfortable. You can choose from the following:

- ▶ nursing bra
- ▶ breast cream
- ▶ breast pads
- ▶ breast pump.

A nursing bra gives extra support and allows easy access during breastfeeding. Most women probably buy two or three and you can choose the sort that opens down the front or the 'drop cup' type. Look for a style with wide shoulder straps and an adjustable back fastening (as the size of your breasts will vary during the day). Get properly fitted for a nursing bra and make sure you feel comfortable and well-supported while wearing it.

The nipples produce their own moisturizing, cleansing fluid during pregnancy and breastfeeding, and therefore breast creams which are formulated to soften and soothe nipples are not an essential. However, if you like using one, then do, but wipe your breasts with a damp tissue and pat them dry before putting your baby to the breast.

Breast pads are useful if your breast milk leaks between feeds, as may happen, especially in the first few weeks. Make sure that you change them frequently to prevent your nipples becoming sore. If you don't want to buy disposable pads, you can get washable, re-usable ones or use clean, folded, cotton handkerchiefs instead.

Breast pumps are primarily used when you want to express your breast milk in order to bottle it for someone else to give to your baby. This is good news if you're a breastfeeding mum who wants the occasional break, but remember to always sterilize the pump before and after use. You can also express by hand and your midwife, health visitor or breastfeeding counsellor will explain how this is done. Expressed breast milk will keep in the fridge for twenty-four hours or you can freeze it for up to three months.

WHAT YOU NEED FOR BOTTLEFEEDING

As well as a supply of baby formula milk, a fully bottlefed baby needs:
- ▶ six bottles, teats and caps
- ▶ sterilizing tank – for four or six bottles
- ▶ sterilizing tablets or sterilizing solution
- ▶ bottle brush
- ▶ plastic knife for levelling scoops of dried formula milk.

You can get by with fewer bottles and teats than this, but getting six means you can make up all or most of your baby's bottle feeds at once and keep them in the fridge ready for use. If you prefer to sterilize by boiling, then you will not need a sterilizing tank or tablets. If you use one of the newer electrical steam sterilizing units, you won't need to use tablets or solution.

CHOOSING BOTTLES AND TEATS

Choose clearly-marked, wide-necked bottles in the appropriate size. For small babies, you can use a small-sized bottle, holding up to 125 millilitres of fluid. This size – and the smaller 60-millilitre size – is also useful for occasional bottles of water or juice. As your baby gets older, you'll need a full-size 250-millilitre bottle.

Teats come with different sized holes, usually small, medium or large. Generally speaking, the younger the baby, the smaller hole size he will need, but you will need to make allowances for your baby's own preference. Some teats have a cross-cut opening instead of an ordinary hole and this allows the baby to control the flow of milk by his own sucking action.

You can choose natural-shaped or traditional-shaped teats. Babies will usually manage with either, but a breastfed baby who needs for some reason to take a bottle may cope better with a natural-shaped one. Ordinary rubber teats wear out after a while and need to be replaced. Clear, silicone teats are longer-lasting and, though they are more expensive initially, they work out cheaper in the long run.

USEFUL EXTRAS

▶ A bottle warmer that plugs into a normal socket and gently warms up your baby's bottle to the temperature you want. It also works with tins and jars of baby food.

▶ A measuring jug is helpful when you want to make up a large quantity of milk at one time, which you can then pour into bottles and store in the fridge to use as required.

STERILIZING EQUIPMENT

It is very important to be scrupulous about sterilizing your baby's bottlefeeding equipment. This is because warm milk is the perfect breeding ground for germs that could make your baby quite ill. You can use the cold water method of sterilizing (shown in the steps below) or sterilize by boiling the equipment in a pan for ten minutes.

HOW TO STERILIZE EQUIPMENT

1. Thoroughly wash all the bottles, teats and other equipment in hot, soapy water. You will need to use a bottle brush to be sure to clear off the milky traces from the insides. Then rinse it all in clean running water.

2. Using clean cold water, fill your sterilizing tank up to the level required and add the correct quantity of tablets or solution. If you use tablets, allow them to dissolve.

3. Put in all your feeding equipment. Make sure everything remains immersed and check that no air bubbles are trapped inside or the equipment will not be thoroughly sterilized. Leave everything in for the specified time. Rinse bottles and teats with cooled boiled water before using, to remove any traces of sterilizing liquid.

STERILIZING TIPS

▶ Teats last longer if they are removed as soon as they have been in the tank for sufficient time. You can keep them in a covered, sterilized jar until needed. Leaving them for prolonged periods in sterilizing liquid will tend to cause the rubber to rot more quickly.
▶ Stand bottles or jugs upright and turn teats and caps upside down in the sterilizing tank to prevent air being trapped.
▶ Never put metal items into the sterilizing tank.

MAKING UP FEEDS

If you are bottlefeeding, it is important to use baby formula milk for at least the first six months of your baby's life. Many experts now feel that whole pasteurized milk should not be used as a drink until the age of nine months or a year (though you can use it in small quantities for mixing and diluting after six months), so stick with the brand of formula milk you used in hospital if it seems to suit your baby. If you are making the switch from breastfeeding or wish to change your brand, ask your health visitor's advice.

HOW TO MAKE UP A FEED

1. Have everything you need to hand. You can either mix the feed directly into the bottle, or you can use a sterilized measuring jug and then pour the made-up feed into the bottle or bottles. Pour the correct amount of freshly-boiled water into the jug or bottle.

2. Using the scoop that comes with the tin or packet of dried formula, add the correct number of scoops to the water. Level off the scoop with a sterilized plastic knife.

3. Stir the powder well so it dissolves in the jug and pour the formula into the bottles. Place the teats and caps on and shake well. If you are making up an individual bottle, put the teat and cap on and shake well to dissolve the formula.

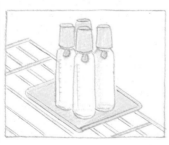

4. If you are making the feed up in advance, store the full bottles, with the teats inverted and the caps on, in the fridge. You can warm each bottle up by standing it in a jug of hot water or by using a bottle warmer (see page 16). If you are going to give a bottle to your baby now, you must cool it down first.

HAVE YOU GOT THE RIGHT TEAT?

Turn the bottle over and give it a shake. The milk should drip from the teat in a steady flow. If it does not, you can either replace the teat with another one with a larger hole, or enlarge the existing hole with a sterilized needle. If your baby seems frustrated, or if he seems to suck a long time to get only a small amount of milk, then the hole may still be too small for him. A baby can get 'windy' sucking on a teat with a hole that is either too small or too big (because the milk flow overwhelms him). Trial and error is the only solution. Bear in mind, too, that teat holes get bigger with repeated use, so you need to be prepared to change.

SAFETY

▶ Remember that the water goes in the jug or bottle first, and then the formula milk powder.

▶ Don't pack the powder into the scoop when you measure it out. Just let it lie naturally and level it off.

▶ Never use a microwave oven to heat your baby's bottle. It will heat the milk to scalding hot yet leave the bottle itself barely warm.

▶ Check the temperature of your baby's feed before giving it to him. Shake a few drops from the teat on to the inside of your wrist. It should feel neither hot nor cold.

▶ Don't keep a half-used warmed bottle in the hope that your baby will want to finish it later. Discard it and use a fresh feed if he seems hungry again.

▶ Wash the bottle and teat straight after the feed, and sterilize them as soon as you can.

▶ Discard teats when they look worn. The surface becomes more difficult to keep clean after repeated use and sterilizing.

▶ If your baby wears a bib during his feed, remove it before putting him down in his cot or pram.

FIRST CUP OR BEAKER

Give your baby the chance to try a cup at about five months. Plastic spouted 'trainer beakers' are best to start with, as they are unbreakable and they bridge the gap between sucking and sipping very well. Few babies manage to use a cup, spouted or not, properly until they are six to eight months or even older, so don't worry if your baby seems slow to master it. It might be worth trying out cups with different-sized holes or choosing one with an adjustable flow, in case the drink is coming out too fast or too slow for him.

Young babies cope best with double-handled or handle-less beakers, before progressing to ones with a single handle. It is useful if the cup is transparent, so your baby can see what he is drinking and you can see how much he has left. A cup with an interchangeable travel lid, or a lid which completely closes sealing the flow holes, allows you to take your baby's drink with you on outings, without getting a puddle at the bottom of your bag!

WHAT YOU WILL NEED FOR WEANING

Once your baby starts his first tastes of solid food, he will need his own set of feeding utensils. This is not absolutely essential (he could use the same as the rest of the family providing you are careful to keep them clean), but items designed for a baby make feedtimes easier and your baby will enjoy recognizing his own special cups, plates and spoons. Whatever you decide to use, you will need:

▶ two plates
▶ spoon (and fork if wanted)
▶ six bibs, at least *or* one or two plastic 'pelican' types.

The easiest plates for babies learning to feed themselves are bowls with high sides. Choose one in an unbreakable material, such as plastic or melamine, as your baby's feeding dish is bound to end up on the floor on occasions, whether by accident or design.

Some bowls have a stay-warm compartment that you fill with hot water, which helps keep your baby's food warm while he is eating it. If you choose this sort, satisfy yourself that the seal keeping in the hot water is firm enough to withstand inquisitive fingers. Suction pads on bowls are an excellent plus, as they stop your baby's dinner sliding around on his tray, which can be most frustrating! As he gets older, you will probably want to change to ordinary bowls, as your baby will be tempted to pull the bowl hard to break the suction – with disastrous results!

For cutlery, small, shallow, plastic spoons are best at first. If you use a fork, a special baby's one with widely-spaced blunt prongs is easy to use and clean.

The more bibs you have the better! At first your baby will need a clean bib at every mealtime, so you do need a pile. Some bibs have a waterproof backing for extra protection. When he is a little older, you could choose a moulded plastic 'pelican' bib with a turned-up pocket for spills that simply rinses clean after every use. Its disadvantage is that some babies find this sort uncomfortable to wear, because of its rigidity. For young babies, a long-sleeved coverall bib protects clothing better than 'front-only' bibs. And for travel or holidays, a packet of disposable bibs could be useful.

INSTANT BABY FOODS OR HOME COOKING?

Commercially-prepared baby foods are normally of good quality and they are certainly convenient. However, they can work out very expensive if you use them all the time. You can give your baby the same food as your family eats, sieved or blended at first, and then mashed or chopped, but remember that babies should not have salted foods and sweetened foods should be kept to a minimum. Home-cooked foods are likely to be more nutritious if you use fresh ingredients and don't over-cook them.

CHOOSING A HIGHCHAIR

Your baby will be happiest on your lap or in his bouncing cradle (see page 44) when taking his very first tastes of solid food. But at around the age of six months, when he is able to sit comfortably, either by himself or with support, he will be ready for a highchair.

Foldaway highchairs used to be rather less attractive than their traditionally-styled counterparts, but that is no longer the case. If you have a small kitchen or eating area, then the convenience of a foldaway may be exactly what you need.

The alternative is a more versatile, non-foldaway, which may offer the option of forming a table-and-lowchair unit and/or incorporate a removable tray that enables the chair to be used at the family dining table. Some chairs convert to a gentle indoor swing, using the same stand as for the highchair position.

More generally, choose a highchair that is easy to clean, without nooks and crannies in the frame or seat where food can lodge. The tray should have a raised rim all the way round to prevent too much of your baby's meal ending up on the floor or in his lap and it is useful if it removes easily for wiping clean. A padded seat is more comfortable than an all-wood or moulded plastic one, though you can buy a special highchair cushion to help with this. Your highchair should have 'D' rings at each side for a safety harness and may also have an integral crotch, or crotch and waist, strap.

For the future, think about a foldaway table seat — it is great for outings and holidays, as it folds up for carrying and clips on to any table surface. It is best used with a baby who can sit up comfortably by himself, but you should never leave your baby unattended in one of these. It must also be used with a separate safety harness.

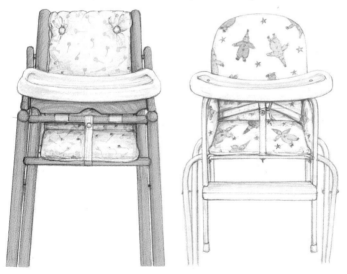

SAFETY

▶ Always secure your baby into his highchair with a separate safety harness (see page 55).
▶ Never leave him alone with food as he could choke.
▶ Don't try to make a swing with a chair that is not specially designed to adapt to this option.

NAPPIES AND NAPPY CHANGING

Although few parents-to-be may actually look forward to changing their baby's nappies, it can become a much pleasanter experience than they expect! It won't take you long to learn how to do it and it can provide a wonderful opportunity for you to talk to and play with your baby. As well as making her clean and comfortable, you can both enjoy the tickling and cuddles that become part of changing time.

You may feel unsure about the 'pleasures' of nappy changing at first, but one thing is certain: you will be doing a lot of it, so it is important to choose the nappy system that suits you, your budget and your growing baby best. The basic choice is between using squares of washable, terry towelling fabric, known as 'terries' or 'terry nappies', or using disposable nappies that your baby uses once and you then throw away. Choosing what is right for you may mean using either terry nappies or disposable nappies all the time – or else deciding to use one method some of the time and switching to the other when you find it more convenient or effective.

TERRIES OR DISPOSABLES?

Terries have been more or less the same for the last generation or two, and they've been tried and trusted by millions of mums and babies over the years. The innovations lie with disposables. Fairly ineffective when first produced, new materials and production methods soon meant that performance improved – but the cost of disposables put them firmly on the 'emergencies only' list for many parents, or else they were regarded as a luxury for use on holidays. Those days are now gone, however – the price of disposable nappies has kept well below inflation, and the effectiveness and fit of all the well-known brands get better all the time.

COST AND CONVENIENCE

So, how do you decide what is best for you? Taking cost as a major factor, terry nappies probably work out cheaper in the long run, especially if you have more than one child. Good-quality terries should see you through at least two children wearing them for at least two years each and the only major expense is the one-off cost of buying them in the first place. However, the overall cost does creep up towards that of disposable nappies because you also need plastic pants, nappy liners, pins, nappy bucket, sterilizer and detergent – plus the electricity needed to machine-wash them, and possibly to tumble dry them. But some of these costs do get swallowed up in your general household expenses to a certain extent and you may not actually notice them! Disposables on the other hand mean a regular and very visible outlay of several pounds per week.

Convenience is another important point. It is a bit of a bore washing and drying nappies, even though washing machines have taken the real drudgery out of it. It is time-consuming and it can be messy, too. Drying terries is especially awkward if you do not have a tumble drier or, at the very least, plenty of space outside to dry them. Even if you have a garden or a balcony with yards of washing line, there will be times in the winter when you cannot use this – and when it seems that every surface in the house is draped with nappies!

Disposables are fresh and clean every time without the nuisance of preparing them – but unless you have them delivered, they do have to be bought and carried home from the shops. If you do not have access to a car, this is an awkward extra bulk to manage on top of your other shopping. And few 'disposables' are actually truly disposable. You need to throw them out with the rest of your household rubbish and a week's worth takes up a lot of room in your dustbin. For hygiene's sake, always seal up the soiled nappies in a plastic bag first – or you can buy special nappy sacks for this (see page 26). There *is* an ecological argument against disposables, not just because of this difficulty in getting rid of them, but also because they are expensive in terms of resources to manufacture.

EFFECTIVENESS AND FIT

What about effectiveness? Terries are very adaptable – after all, with practised folding, one size really does fit all, from the tiniest newborn to the most strapping three-year-old. With the right-fitting plastic pants, you can get a pretty good seal round front, back and legs. The best have a good absorbency and, as long as the plastic pants are not too tight, a terry nappy is comfortable for a baby to wear as the fabric has natural 'give' in it. Even so, modern all-in-one disposables are more absorbent than terries, on the whole, and they keep your baby's skin dry because the moisture is prevented from seeping back to the surface of the nappy. Once you have found the right size and shape for your baby – and you will probably need to shop around from time to time as your baby grows to find what is best for her – the fit should be almost as good as a terry nappy with waterproof pants. For many people, an all-in-one disposable is easier than a terry to put on and achieve a good fit.

TERRY NAPPIES

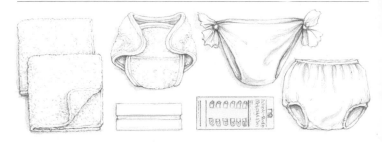

If you decide that terry nappies are the best option for you and your baby, this is what you will need:

▶ twenty-four terry towelling nappies, at least
▶ four pairs of waterproof pants, at least
▶ box of disposable nappy liners
▶ card of nappy pins
▶ toiletries (see page 27)
▶ nappy bucket with lid
▶ nappy sanitizing powder.

Terry nappies are available in different absorbencies. The thicker and denser the looped pile of the fabric, the more wetness the nappy will hold. Generally speaking, most manufacturers have two or three different nappies in their ranges: the more expensive the nappy, the better the absorbency. It will pay you to get the best nappies you can afford, as the thicker nappies withstand constant washing and using for longer, and they tend to need changing less frequently.

If you intend to use terry nappies the whole time, even if you plan on switching to disposables later on, you will need at least two dozen. Less than this and you will find it very difficult to keep up with the washing and drying.

You can buy specially-shaped nappies in double-thickness towelling which save folding. However, they do take longer to dry than normal squares and they can't be adapted to the size of your baby.

For night-time use, and for older children who still need a nappy at night, you can buy extra-absorbent, larger-sized nappies. These could be very useful for the 'heavy wetting' baby who sleeps through the night, but who ends up soaked in the morning (though you can put a double nappy on her instead).

Waterproof pants can make all the difference between providing an effective nappy and one that leaks at the edges, so fit is important. However, you need to choose one with a bit of 'give' round the legs and waistline, or your baby will get sore, chafed skin. More expensive pants give a longer life and remain softer for longer after repeated washing. Cheaper ones will harden and tear after a short time. You can choose pull-on pants with elasticated waist and legs, tie-on pants (though it can be difficult to cover all the nappy effectively with these) or pants with popper closings at the waist and legs. Frilly pants, coloured or patterned ones, are smarter than ordinary ones.

Nappy liners help draw moisture away from your baby's skin and they also 'catch' the worst of any soiling. You do not have to use disposable ones; you can choose washable ones or use a folded-up muslin square instead.

Nappy pins are essential items, as they have a cover for the head to prevent accidental unclosing.

FOLDING A TERRY NAPPY

You can experiment to find the best fit for your baby and your midwife or health visitor will be happy to show you some ideas. This is one of the most popular methods.

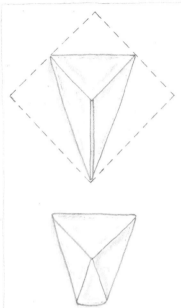

The kite – suitable for boys and girls and easily adjustable to the size of your baby.

1. Place the nappy in front of you 'diamond fashion'. Bring the top point and the two side points to the centre to make a kite shape.

2. Fold the bottom point upwards and adjust it, making the nappy shorter or longer, to fit your baby.

TERRY NAPPY CARE

It is important to keep your baby's terries (and washable liners if used) clean and free from bacteria by soaking them in sanitizing solution after use. Make up the solution in a bucket, following the instructions on the packet. After rinsing off any soiling in the lavatory, place used nappies in the bucket, leave for the required time and then rinse to remove all traces of the solution. Stained nappies will need washing. Some parents prefer to use two buckets, one for wet nappies (which should just need rinsing) and the other for soiled nappies. Another method of sanitizing is to boil the nappies, but most people find this less convenient than soaking.

TERRY TIPS

▶ A special night-time nappy or two nappies worn at once may save you doing an extra change at night.
▶ Avoid washing waterproof pants on a hot wash – it will shorten their life considerably.
▶ After drying, fold clean terries so that they are ready to use at nappy changing time.

DISPOSABLE NAPPIES

If the convenience of disposables suits you best, you will need:
- ▶ pack of disposable all-in-ones
- ▶ toiletries (see opposite)
- ▶ plastic bags or nappy sacks.

The type of disposable nappy most widely used these days is an all-in-one which combines a highly absorbent lining with a waterproof outer layer. The nappy fixes with self-adhesive tapes at the sides. On most makes of all-in-one, these tapes are resealable – the tabs come in two parts. You can peel back the top half to check the nappy and refasten it if the nappy is clean and dry.

Most sorts of disposables are available in different sizes and this, together with the fact that you can adjust the self-adhesive tapes across your baby's middle, means that you can usually achieve a reasonably good fit. New manufacturing processes have made today's all-in-ones highly efficient and comfortable for babies to wear. Some sorts have a printed 'wetness indicator' on the outside, which shows you when your baby needs changing, and some are made of a special material that absorbs urine without allowing it to seep back to the lining – and this means your baby's skin stays drier longer, reducing the risk of nappy rash.

You can get bulk quantities of disposable nappies delivered to your door, and although this means a large expense all in one go, it does save the bother of buying and carrying home. Ask at your Mothercare store or look in your newspaper for services advertised locally.

DISPOSING OF THE DISPOSABLE

Getting rid of disposable nappies may pose a problem, as only the insert sort can be flushed away. The hygienic way to dispose of nappies is to first rinse off any heavy soiling in the lavatory. Then roll the nappy up, soiled/wet side inwards, and secure with the tapes which should still have a bit of 'stick' on them. Finally, place the nappy in a bag (a special plastic nappy sack is ideal), knot the top and place in the bin.

TIP FOR DISPOSABLES

▶ Make sure your hands are dry and free from grease or the tapes will not stick.

SAFETY

▶ Store plastic bags or nappy sacks somewhere well out of your baby's reach.

NAPPY CHANGING TIPS

▶ You can help make changing fun for an older, wriggly baby who resents being put on her back and manhandled by having one or two small toys you keep especially for nappy time.

▶ A baby boy may give you a surprise shower during a nappy change. You can be prepared by placing a nappy or towel over his front.

▶ Always keep a nappy sack or plastic bag (for the soiled nappy) in the changing bag, plus a spare nappy and small-size toiletries. Then you are prepared at any time just to pick up your bag and go, without needing to pack it specially every time.

TOILETRIES

There are lots of different toiletries available to help with nappy changing and it can be difficult to sort out which does what. You basically need something to clean your baby's bottom and something to protect it against soreness. You will soon discover what you find most useful. Keep a supply of these toiletries in your layette basket, baby box or changing bag so that you always have them to hand.

▶ Baby wipes: disposable wipes, premoistened with a cleansing fluid or lotion. Ideal for cleaning and protecting your baby's skin and very useful when you're out and about.

▶ Baby lotion: use with cotton wool or tissues for cleaning your baby's bottom.

▶ Baby cream: for applying after cleaning, to act as a barrier and to protect skin from nappy rash. Some types – for example, zinc and castor oil cream and special nappy rash creams – will speed up healing if there is a rash or other soreness already present.

▶ Cotton wool: in a roll, pleats or balls.

▶ Tissues: as an alternative to cotton wool.

You may prefer to use plain warm water to clean your baby's bottom and this may be gentler to her skin if she has a rash. It is important to apply some form of cream or barrier between the nappy and your baby's skin, however, at least until your baby is older and 'tougher'. Nappy rash – a result of bacteria forming from urine and stools – is painful, and regular applications of cream can help avoid it. If, however, your baby's bottom does become very sore, you may need to take her to the doctor who will prescribe an ointment for soothing her skin and clearing up any infection.

WHERE TO CHANGE – AND WHAT WILL HELP

You can change your baby on a towel or changing mat placed on a clean surface, such as a table top, baby dresser or cot, on your lap or on the floor. You should remain with your baby all the time if she is on a raised surface, in case she falls off. In fact, once your baby is able to roll, she is only really safe on your lap or on the floor while being changed or dressed.

A baby dresser is useful, though not essential, as it can store close at hand all you need for changing and dressing, as well as providing a surface your baby can lie on.

A changing mat provides a clean, padded, wipe-down surface that you can also use at bathtimes. For out and about, think about buying a changing bag – one with plenty of room, plus its own changing mat, or one that unzips to form a mat itself – for carrying all the equipment you need when away from home. For use at home, a layette basket or a baby box for bathtime and nappy-changing needs can be carried from room to room quite easily.

HOW OFTEN TO CHANGE?

Most young babies need changing at every feed, although if your baby is feeding 'little and often' it may not be necessary every time. You may need to give her extra changes, though, if her nappy leaks between feeds or if she soils her nappy.

HOW TO CHANGE YOUR BABY'S NAPPY

1. Clean your baby's bottom with some cotton wool and warm water or baby lotion or a baby wipe. Apply baby cream if you use it.

2. Slip the clean folded nappy under her bottom, bring the narrow end up between her legs and fold the sides over the top.

3. With one hand protecting her tummy, pin all three pieces with a nappy pin. Put on waterproof pants.

All-in-one disposable
Slip the end with the sticky tapes under her bottom, peel the tapes from their backing and fix at the front of the nappy.

LOOKING AHEAD TO POTTY TRAINING

These days, most parents are happy to leave potty training until much nearer their child's second birthday, but when the time comes to think about it, make sure the potty you choose feels stable and sturdy. An alternative is a potty chair, with a lift-out inner bowl that you remove for emptying and washing. Some older toddlers may prefer a special lavatory training seat which fits over the big seat enabling them to use the lavatory. A 'grow-tall' step will help your child climb on the seat and can also be used by a boy to stand at the lavatory.

BATHTIME

Bathing and washing can be enjoyable for both you and your baby – though you will be quite normal if you feel very awkward at first, and even a bit nervous, especially about giving your baby a bath. Take heart, though, you will get a lot better with practice.

Don't be too worried about giving your baby a regular bath in the first few weeks. There is normally no real urgency to give your baby his first bath in the day or so after birth, either, unless you want to, and most maternity units and midwives are very flexible about this.

However, very new babies do need at least a morning wash, or 'top and tail', and as your baby gets older you will probably want to give him an evening wash as well, if not a bath every night.

When you do start bathing, just aim to do it once every few days or so. If you manage this, and top and tail at least once on the days that you do not bath him, your baby will be fine.

WHERE AND WHEN TO BATH YOUR BABY

Any warm room will be fine to bath your baby in, though it might be easiest for you if you're close to taps and a sink or bath for filling and emptying. Bathrooms in some houses can be cold, however, so if you feel the living room or bedroom is warmer, take the baby bath in there and put towels down on the floor to absorb splashes.

There is no special time of the day that you must bath your baby. Babies are naturally unpredictable in the early weeks and if you decide that you will bath him at ten o'clock or six o'clock, for instance, you will have to accept that there are bound to be occasions when you will not manage such precise timings! Your baby is quite likely to be asleep or you may find that you have more pressing tasks on hand. However, until your baby is a little older it is a good idea to try and avoid times when he has just been fed (he is likely to be sleepy and the picking up and handling may upset him or even make him a bit sick) and when he is hungry (bathing him instead of feeding him will make him very cross!). Sometimes parents find a good time to

▶   See page 34 for bathing your baby

bath is in the evenings when babies may be a little crotchety without actually being hungry or sleepy. Bathing can be quite soothing and settling for a baby in this sort of mood.

Nevertheless, as your baby grows, establishing a reasonably regular bathtime can be a help in making your day with your baby a bit more organized. A bath in the evening, followed by a feed, can become a soothing and reliable way to get your baby off to sleep. Alternatively, you might find it best to bath your baby in the mornings, after the rest of the household has left for school or work.

TOPPING AND TAILING

You will be shown how to top and tail either in hospital or at home by your community midwife when she visits you. Topping and tailing is a quick and efficient way of getting your baby clean and fresh, without going through the whole bathtime routine. You can top and tail your baby wherever is most convenient for you, but do make sure the room you are in is warm and free from draughts. You will need:

- ▶ changing mat
- ▶ towel
- ▶ cotton wool: in a roll, balls or pleats
- ▶ cotton wool swabs, if used
- ▶ bowl of warm water or plastic 'top and tail' bowl
- ▶ baby cream
- ▶ round-ended nail scissors
- ▶ clean nappy
- ▶ clean clothing, if necessary.

HOW TO TOP AND TAIL

1. Take off your baby's outer clothing, leaving his vest and nappy on. With a small piece of cotton wool dipped in warm water, clean his eyes, from the inside corner to the outside, using a fresh piece for each eye. Dry each eye with a clean piece of cotton wool.

2. Do the same for each ear, taking care not to poke anything inside – just wipe away what you can see. Wash and dry the rest of your baby's face, neck and hands. Check whether his nails need cutting.

3. Remove his nappy and clean his bottom (see page 29). Put on a clean nappy and dress him.

▶ *See page 29 for changing your baby*

CHOOSING A BABY BATH

Most people buy a baby bath of some sort, even if it's just a washing-up bowl for use in the very first weeks! If you decide to buy a 'proper' baby bath, though, consider buying a stand with it as well. This saves aches and strain on your back, and it can be folded away neatly when not in use.

Look for useful features such as a toiletries shelf to keep the soap and other washing items handy. If the shelf is removable, you can lift it out to give more room as your baby grows. A removable backrest will give support to your baby's back while he is small and help keep his head out of the water, allowing you to have your hands free. Remember never to leave him unattended, though, and remove the backrest when your baby is older and can sit up. A textured inner surface to the bath will help avoid slips and slides, or use a non-slip baby bath mat with it (see page 61).

Some families, however, decide to do without a baby bath, and the new baby is put in the big bath from the start. This is fine, but bear in mind that you will need more water than in a baby bath and you may find that all that bending puts a strain on your back. If you have a toddler, you can either bath your baby before his big brother or sister (at first, it is kinder to bath the baby on his own so he does not risk getting splashed) or, later, at the same time.

If you like, you can take your baby into the bath with you instead, though you will need to be careful to lower the temperature of the water to suit him. It is safest if your partner or someone else is there to hand the baby to you when you're already in the bath so you'll have both hands free to hold him securely.

TIPS

▶ You can put the baby bath in the big bath and bath your baby there if you like, for easy filling.
▶ Don't overfill the baby bath – there should be just enough water to keep your baby's body immersed as you support his head and shoulders out of the water.
▶ Make sure the stand and bath you buy are made to go together.

WHAT ELSE YOU NEED FOR BABY'S BATHTIME

Once you've decided where to bath your baby, you'll want to consider what other items you need. Choose from this checklist:

- ▶ jug or bowl – filled with warm water for rinsing your baby's scalp
- ▶ sponge, preferably natural
- ▶ two flannels/wash cloths
- ▶ soap – use a pure, unscented and uncoloured type while your baby is young
- ▶ baby bathcare liquid – replaces soap and mixes straight into the water to make a gently cleansing solution

- ▶ shampoo – only needed for babies with a considerable amount of hair; use a mild baby variety that may be available as an easy-to-use mousse.
- ▶ cotton wool – for cleaning your baby's face and ears.
- ▶ two towels – a hooded towelling cuddle robe is a cosy and warm alternative to one of the towels
- ▶ baby oil – to massage gently on to your baby's skin after the bath, if wanted

- ▶ baby powder – to use after thoroughly drying your baby, if wanted
- ▶ changing mat
- ▶ baby cream
- ▶ soft hairbrush
- ▶ clean nappy (plus waterproof pants and nappy pins, if used)
- ▶ clean clothing.

SAFETY

▶ Have everything ready before you start, so you don't have to leave your baby even for a short while.

▶ Never leave your baby unattended in the bath for even a moment – he could easily drown. If you need to answer the phone or the door – or fetch something you have forgotten – take your baby with you, well wrapped up in a towel to keep him warm.

▶ Make sure the room in which you bath your baby is warm and draught-free.

▶ Always run the cold water in the bath first, and then add the hot. Doing it this way round means that the bottom of the bath does not get too hot and you are less likely to scald your baby.

▶ Mix the water in the jug or bowl (for washing your baby's face and rinsing his scalp) in the same way.

▶ Always check the temperature of the water with your elbow before putting your baby in the bath. It should feel pleasantly warm.

▶ A non-slip bathmat in the big bath will help your baby feel more confident and secure – as well as making him less likely to slip over when he can sit.

▶ If you like to use baby powder after the bath, shake it into your hand first and then apply it, so you don't shower your baby with it.

▶ *See page 31 for topping and tailing*

BATHING YOUR BABY

Remember to act as if you are confident, even if you don't feel it! A firm, gentle hold on your baby will help him feel secure – and it's also a lot safer, of course. You will probably be shown how to bath your baby by your midwife in hospital, the community midwife at home or your health visitor. You may like them to do this for you or prefer them to watch while you do it for the very first time. Remember there is no one perfect way to bath a baby – you can choose the particular method and order that suits you, and as long as you are safe, sensible and hygienic there is not a lot that can go wrong.

Make sure before you start that you have everything you need near at hand. You can fill your baby bath either direct from the tap, if you can manage it without too much risk of slopping water about as you lift it away, or use jugs of water. Whatever you do, remember the golden rule: always pour in cold water first and *then* hot. After filling the bath, add baby bathcare liquid if you're using it. Keep a jug of warm water to one side for rinsing your baby's head.

HOW TO BATH YOUR BABY

1. Undress your baby, wrap him in a towel and wash his face, as in topping and tailing on page 31. Supporting his back and head, wash his scalp, rinse it using the jug of warm water and gently pat his head dry.

2. Clean his bottom and if you are using soap, gently lather it all over his body. Carefully lift your baby into the bath (remember that he'll be slippery if you've used soap), supporting him under his shoulders with one of your arms and grasping his far upper arm with your hand.

3. Now rinse off the soap by gently scooping water over him with your hand. If you are using babycare liquid, just swish the water round his body.

4. Lift your baby out and wrap him in a towel or hooded robe to stop him getting cold. Use the other towel to dry him all over, particularly in the little creases at the tops of his thighs and round his neck. Apply baby cream and powder, if used. Put on a clean nappy and clothes.

BATHING YOUR OLDER BABY

As your baby gets older, bathtime really does become fun. Your baby will begin to enjoy the sensation of the water against his skin and the feeling of freshness and well-being he gets afterwards. It is a good idea to incorporate the bath into your baby's daily routine (see Where and when to bath your baby, page 30) when you can. As well as helping to structure the day for you, it gives you both a special time together, when he knows he can enjoy your undivided attention.

If you have always used a baby bath, then you will have to make the change to the family bath at some time. When exactly you do this is up to you. One suggestion would be to try it when the baby bath becomes too small for your baby to enjoy playing with the water. This could be from around four or five months old, depending on his size and that of your bath. Or perhaps you would prefer to wait until your baby is able to sit up comfortably without support, to save the strain on your back – and that could mean not until seven or eight months. Do remember that you should always stay with your baby, even when he's able to sit on his own – he could so easily slip and drown.

Once you have decided to make the move, you could try putting the baby bath into the big bath a couple of times and bathing your baby like this, so you can make the change a little more gradual. Be guided by your baby, however. If he is the sort that is unlikely to be frightened by the big bath, perhaps because he has already been in it with you, then you may not need to make this transitional step.

BATHTIME IS PLAYTIME!

Pouring and floating toys will help your baby make the most of this great opportunity to learn about water and what it can do. You can add sponges, plastic beakers and spoons from the kitchen to the toys you buy – and don't forget fun with bubble bath liquid. Choose a mild, children's brand, as stronger types might irritate your baby's skin. A special net bag, hung between the taps, keeps toys out of the way.

MY BABY HATES THE BIG BATH!

This is quite a common problem, but it's one that rarely lasts. If your baby becomes obviously frightened at bathtime, then think of other ways of keeping him clean for the time being. Try putting him back in the baby bath or just washing him all over with a bowl of warm water. Encourage him to play with the water, by swirling it round and sailing small toys on it. When you decide to try the bath again, make bathtime brief and be especially careful not to splash water on your baby's face as this may upset him.

BEDTIME

One of the first things you will need to think about is where your baby will sleep. You may want her in her own room or you may plan to have her sleep with you in your room, at least at first, to make night feeds easier. You may want to consider having a different sleeping place for her during the day or you may decide to put her in the same place both day and night.

If you have a very noisy household, then your baby may be best off sleeping in her room (or wherever she sleeps at night) for daytime naps, so she doesn't get woken up unnecessarily. On the other hand, most new babies sleep very soundly and your baby will usually wake up if she is hungry or uncomfortable, rather than if she is disturbed by noise. While your baby is at this stage (and it doesn't last beyond the first few months), it might be easiest for you to let her sleep during the day in the pram or carrycot, if you have one. This way, if you want to go out shopping or to visit friends, you can simply wheel or carry her out without having to disturb her.

When it comes to night-time, some parents actually dislike sharing their room with the baby. It may be partly because they find it difficult to relax and 'switch off' when they are aware of the baby and are perhaps worried by any minor change in breathing or snuffling. Other parents don't mind this and prefer to know their baby is near. It really is up to you – and your baby. Some babies sleep better when on their own; others find the loneliness quite upsetting, even at a very young age. Don't feel you are starting up 'bad habits' by having your baby in your room, or even your bed, if that is what gives everybody the best possible night's sleep. You may set up a pattern, but it's not one that is impossible to break at a later stage. If you don't want your baby sleeping in the same room as you, but worry that you will not hear her if she cries, consider installing a baby alarm (see page 60).

YOUR BABY'S ROOM

Whether your baby has her own room, or just a corner of yours, is not important. You do need to be sure that the room can be kept warm, especially while your baby is young and relatively inactive. For a new baby, the recommended room temperature is 20 °C (68°F).

If your baby does have her own room, it can be very enjoyable to decorate it and furnish it to suit her needs.

DECORATING THE ROOM

If you choose paint for the walls (or furniture), make sure that it is lead-free. Bear in mind that paint is easier to keep clean than wallpaper, unless you buy a washable one. Washable papers are available in a wide variety of colours and designs, but if this is your choice, think about what your child might like in a few years' time. You don't want anything too babyish, unless you're happy to re-decorate quite soon.

There are also excellent ranges of co-ordinating prints for wallpaper, bedding, lampshades, curtains and wall friezes. By carefully selecting what you want, you can create a really smart-looking room without spending a lot of money. For flooring, think about washable cork tiles, brightened with a non-slip, washable rug.

FURNISHINGS

As well as a cot and a comfortable chair for you to sit on to feed, you will need sensible storage in your baby's room. At first, a chest of drawers will be fine, as you won't need any hanging space for your baby's clothing for a year or two. Baby dressers and changing units (see page 28) are worth considering, as they provide useful storage space for clothes and nappies.

Open shelving used to store small items such as books and toiletries keeps them easily accessible. Think about where to keep your baby's toys: a chest or a blanket box is one idea, and it will go on providing useful linen storage after your child no longer needs it.

HEATING AND LIGHTING

Your baby's room needs to be warm. If the room isn't centrally heated, you must find a safe way of keeping up the temperature when necessary. A convector heater is ideal – make sure the one you choose carries a BEAB (British Electrotechnical Approvals Board) safety mark. If you have to use an electric or gas fire, or an open fire, you must have a fireguard (see page 60).

As your baby grows, she will become better able to regulate her own temperature effectively, and as long as she has adequate bedding and clothing, it won't matter if her room gets cooler during the night.

Keep your baby's cot and changing area away from an overhead light and think about installing a dimmer switch. You can then lower the light at night, thereby disturbing your baby less. A nightlight or a glow light (see Safe lighting, page 59) may also help.

BRIGHT AND EASY TOUCHES

▶ Stick a pretty frieze round the walls – or hand-paint a stencil.
▶ Hang a mobile from the ceiling.
▶ Cover some floor cushions in the same fabric as the curtains. They're great for rough and tumble play later on!
▶ Choose a lampshade covered in a nursery fabric.

SAFETY

▶ If you use a free-standing lamp, keep any trailing flex away from where you might trip over it and place the lamp well out of reach of your baby's cot. When your baby starts to crawl, put the lamp away until she's older.
▶ Make sure that any mobile is well out of your baby's reach.

BABY'S FIRST BED

Although you can put your baby straight into a full-size cot (see opposite), many families prefer to use something smaller for the first few months. Apart from the fact that it is almost traditional to do so, a smaller sleeping place can be cosier for the baby and fairly portable, so you can move it from room to room when necessary. Do remember that none of the following is an essential, though, and your baby may use her first bed for as little as three months, depending on its size and her rate of growth.

If you choose to use a carrycot (see page 51) as your baby's first bed you will extend its use beyond the early months if you buy a transporter with it that converts it to wheeled transport for use outside. Alternatively, you can use it with a stand, if you like, for indoor use.

A Moses basket looks beautiful, especially when it's draped and frilled. You can also buy a stand for the basket. A wooden cradle or crib can look lovely, too, and if you choose the sort which rocks or swings, you may find it helpful in soothing your baby to sleep.

FIRST BEDDING

Although your baby may not use her crib or basket for very long, the bedding you buy for it – apart from the mattress – may have a longer life as pram, carrycot or traveller bedding. You will need:

▶ waterproof mattress
▶ four sheets, at least
▶ two blankets, at least
▶ one top cover or quilt, at least.

SAFETY

▶ Never give a pillow to a baby under one year old.
▶ Make sure that the stand or transporter you choose is made to go with the Moses basket or carrycot and fits properly.
▶ Check that the inside of a Moses basket is fitted with securely attached fabric, so there is no rough surface.
▶ Check that a cot is well-made and

stable with no awkward corners or joints where your baby's tiny limbs might get trapped.
▶ The dropside mechanism should be secure and too difficult for a child to operate.
▶ There should be no horizontal bars that could be used as a ladder by an active climber.
▶ Paintwork should be lead-free and non-toxic.

YOUR BABY'S COT

If your baby is not in a cot from the start, she will need one by the time she is six months at the latest, depending on when she has grown out of her first bed. You can choose from several different and useful features including:

▶ drawers underneath to give extra storage space

▶ a cabinet attached to the end for storage

▶ a dropside, to make lifting your baby in and out easier

▶ an adjustable height mattress – use its highest position when your baby is small, lower it as soon as your baby can sit up.

Any of these extra features are likely to make your cot more expensive than the most basic model, of course. You are also likely to pay more for a cot with a curved or shaped outline, or where there is any decorative turning on the wood.

An alternative to a traditional cot is a cot bed – a larger-than-usual cot that converts to a child-size bed when you need it. This is good value for money, even though you pay more at the outset, as it can be used until your child is about six years old. If you plan on having any more children, however, your first child might be in the bed when you need it again for a cot – and you'll end up having to buy either a new bed or a cot anyway.

SECOND-HAND SAFETY

Cots are a popular item to pass down the family, but some older cots may be unsafe. Check very carefully that:

▶ the dropside mechanism has no obtruding screw heads (these could catch on clothing and cause strangulation)

▶ the mattress fits exactly – in fact, it's safer and more hygienic to buy a new mattress

▶ the cot is not on castors

▶ all the bars are securely fixed and the distance between each one measures not less than 25mm (1in) and not more than 60mm (2½in)

▶ the wood is free from splinters

▶ there is no transfer picture or peeling paint on the inside which might be picked off and eaten

▶ any paint or varnish you use on the cot is lead-free.

BEDDING FOR THE COT

Some new cots are sold with a mattress; others are not. Either way, you will need to make sure the mattress is the right size and shape, leaving no gaps where a tiny arm or leg could get caught. Most cots – though not all – are in a standard size and will take a standard mattress, so you're unlikely to have a problem.

You will need a mattress that is waterproof or that has one waterproof side. Depending on how much you want to spend, you could choose a basic foam-filled mattress, a mattress with a vented head-section for extra safety, or a mattress with a sprung interior.

For additional protection, you can buy waterproof sheets to place over the cot mattress. The safest type have tie-on tapes or elasticated sides to prevent them slipping off the mattress.

SHEETS AND COVERS

For your baby's cot you will need, in addition to the mattress:

▶ four sheets, at least – fitted ones cost more, but they are worth it for the extra comfort they give your baby and the ease with which you can straighten her bedding

▶ a duvet and two covers *or* two blankets or covers, at least.

Today's cot duvet covers come in exciting and colourful designs – and if you choose one that is reversible (with a different print on the other side) you get two looks for the price of one! They make cot-making a lot easier, too.

As well as this basic bedding, you can buy cot bumpers, which prevent your baby hurting her head against the bars as she sleeps (some very active babies need two sets – one for the top end of the cot and one for the bottom). A set of drapes for the cot can make it look pretty special, too.

TOYS, MOBILES AND MUSIC

It is worthwhile helping your baby to think of her cot as a pleasant, comforting place to be, right from the start. Try putting safe toys in or on the cot so she will grow to know them and enjoy looking at them.

A cot mobile, fixed to the non-dropside of her cot, will fascinate your baby as she watches its gentle movement. It's especially nice if the mobile is a musical one, so she can drift off to sleep while listening to a familiar tune. Attach it where she can easily see it, but well out of her reach. Look for cot toys that are specially designed to fix on to the cot bars, where they can be played with, but not thrown out! She'll like having one or two soft toys for company, too.

PUTTING YOUR BABY DOWN TO SLEEP

It is comforting to some babies, especially when they're small, to be wrapped up firmly in a shawl or sheet before being put down in the cot. You can also prepare the room by having a low light on (see Lighting, page 37). Always put a young baby down to sleep on her tummy or her side – never on her back – just in case she brings up any milk. Many babies get a lot of comfort from familiar blankets, cloths or soft toys – it is generally the texture that appeals to them at first, though as they grow older the thing, whatever it is, is loved just for itself! If you notice your baby getting very attached to something, it may be a sensible move to get another identical item, so you can pop the other one in the wash from time to time.

TRAVEL COTS

If you plan to holiday with your baby, or to visit friends, then a travel cot is worth considering. It is not hard-wearing enough to stand up to several years of everyday use, however, so don't buy one as an alternative to a normal cot.

Check when you are buying one that it is light enough for you to carry and compact enough when folded to make storage no problem. Very shallow cots are not suitable for older babies and toddlers; if you want the cot to suit a wider age range, then choose a fairly deep one.

SAFETY

▶ Remember to replace a cot mattress if the outer covering shows sign of tearing, in case the filling should come out.

▶ Make sure that a cot bumper ties only at the top of the cot (not near the mattress too) and that the ties are no longer than 30cm (1ft).

▶ Never hang a mobile directly above your child's face or within her reach, and once she can sit up in her cot, remove it.

▶ Check that any soft toys in the cot have no ribbons or loose parts.

YOUR DAY WITH YOUR BABY

Newborn babies spend a great deal of time feeding and sleeping at first, though 'settling problems', when your baby finds it difficult to drop off to a restful, long-lasting sleep after feeding, are not at all uncommon. As time goes on, however, your baby is likely to have times of the day when he isn't hungry and he isn't tired. Babies vary a great deal in the amount of attention they need at these times, and the same baby may behave very differently at different stages and at different times in the day! For instance, your baby may be very wakeful in the evenings and seem to need a lot of one-to-one attention. And yet in the mornings, he may be quite content to lie in a bouncing cradle (see page 44), just watching you.

If you have work to do about the house and don't want to keep moving your baby and his chair from room to room, you may find a baby sling or carrier useful (see page 45). This holds him comfortably and securely against your front leaving your hands free to do other things. Your baby will love the warmth and closeness, and you can chat to him as you get on with preparing the lunch or sorting the washing. At other times he can lie on a playmat or rug on the floor and will enjoy kicking his legs for a while, provided he can still see you.

It is a good idea to try and get out of the house at least once a day with your baby. Don't make it an unbreakable rule; as with everything to do with a baby, you need to be flexible and not a slave to routines and schedules. Both of you will benefit from the fresh air and, as long as you have dressed and wrapped him appropriately for the weather, he won't come to any harm. Even on the coldest, most blustery days, a small baby can be well-protected in a pram, traveller or carrycot, with a cosy shawl, one or two blankets or a quilt, and the rain cover buttoned on. On very hot days, use a sunshade attached to your stroller, pushchair or pram and cover your baby loosely with a sheet to protect his skin from the sun.

Use these outings as a means of meeting other mothers. You may chat to other mothers while pram-pushing in the local park or meet them on a more regular basis at a coffee morning or a mother and baby group. While small babies are too young to derive much benefit from these social activities, they are a good opportunity for you to get to know other mothers and to discuss common interests.

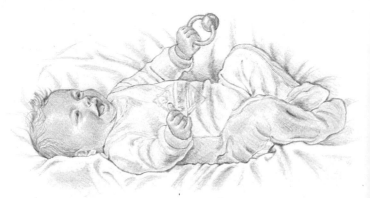

ENTERTAINING YOUR BABY

Your baby will find delight in the simplest things around him. Everything is new and fascinating and he'll love it if you walk him round the room and let him look at different things. Talk to him about what he's looking at – sometimes you'll find something that really seems to absorb him for some minutes, such as a branch waving outside the window. Babies love gentle movement, either watching it or feeling it, and they adore being talked and sung to. As he gets a little older, he'll be able to hold on to objects such as rattles, small toys or safe household items like plastic spoons.

Don't expect your baby's interest to be captured for very long. Some babies do get bored quite quickly and need a change after only a very short time. Others are more 'thoughtful' and placid and may be more likely to stay interested in the same thing. Remember that babies enjoy exploring texture and shape as well, so keep a variety of different safe things to give him, one at a time. Don't surround your baby with too many objects at once. He may get confused and be unable to play with anything for very long. Just bring out one or two toys at a time and then swap them for other things when he loses interest in them.

YOUR BABY MAY ENJOY LOOKING AT:

▶ his hands
▶ his feet
▶ your face
▶ his own reflection, and yours as you hold him and talk to him, in the mirror
▶ other babies and toddlers
▶ the scene outside the window
▶ clothes tumbling round in the washing machine
▶ bubbles being blown
▶ pictures in a book – the bolder and clearer the better

YOUR BABY MAY ENJOY HEARING:

▶ your singing
▶ other babies' and toddlers' chatter and laughter
▶ voices on the radio
▶ taped music
▶ a tune from a musical box
▶ a tinkling bell
▶ a rattle or squeaker

COPING WITH CRYING

Continuous, unexplained crying may be caused by illness, so if you are worried, do ask your doctor to check that your baby is well. Some babies, however, just do cry a lot and it can create a great deal of stress for parents. If your baby is one of these, take heart – they do grow out of it!

For occasional bouts of crying, there are a number of fairly obvious checks to make, such as whether your baby is hungry, too hot or too cold, as well as looking for the infamous open nappy pin! If you think it could be hunger, try feeding him more frequently. Some babies need feeding 'little and often' and may also get comfort from sucking. If your baby is bottlefed, make his feeds smaller and more frequent – for example, instead of giving him five bottles a day, divide his total intake into eight bottles.

Another idea to try might be to get out of the house more often. Most babies are soothed by the motion of your walk or by the rhythm of being wheeled along in a pram or pushchair.

BABY'S FIRST SEAT

Right from the start, your baby can be placed in his own special baby seat. For even very young babies, it is a great chance to lean back comfortably and safely, while also having a good view of everything that is going on. Although a seat like this is not an absolute essential, it is a much safer place to 'park' your baby than propped up on a sofa – and even the most placid of babies gets bored lying in a cot or pram while awake. You'll find once you have a baby seat that your baby will probably use it every day.

A bouncing cradle is a baby-sized lightweight seat, suitable for babies up to the age of about six months (when most get to be too big for it). Your baby is held snugly by a waist and crotch strap. Even a very slight movement causes a gentle rocking motion and many babies learn to bounce the cradle all by themselves. Most bouncing cradles pack flat when not in use.

An alternative to a bouncing cradle is a sturdy baby rocker, with a lined, rigid seat whose angle you can adjust according to your baby's age – further back for a young baby, more upright as he gets older. Some baby rockers can be converted to a non-rocking stable low chair, by turning the rocking frame over.

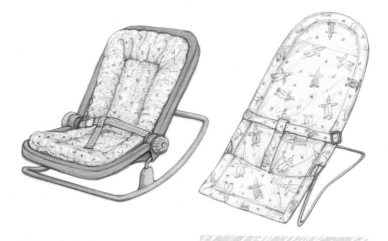

SAFETY

▶ Never leave your baby unsupervised in a rocker or a cradle, and never use it on a raised surface. Always place it on the floor.

▶ Always check that the baby carrier is properly adjusted and securely fastened.

▶ Always put a safety harness on your baby when he is sitting in the kiddy carrier.

▶ Never leave your baby alone in the kiddy carrier and don't use it as a free-standing seat.

USEFUL EXTRAS

▶ A bouncing cradle toy can fit across the front of the bouncing cradle or rocker, within easy reach of your baby's hands.

▶ A wipe-clean playmat inside the floor of a wooden playpen makes a softer landing for your baby and helps keep the floor of the playpen clean. It can also be used to catch spills under your baby's highchair at mealtimes.

▶ A hooded cape that fits over your baby in the carrier keeps him warm and dry in bad weather.

PLAYPENS

Not every family needs a playpen – and it has to be said, some babies are only in them a short while before they start to make loud objections! – but for many, a playpen provides a useful, safe haven for a baby. They are often used as an evening and night-time storage place for toys, as well.

Your baby can be popped into the playpen if you need to answer the door or the phone, or he can play quite happily there for a while, allowing you to get on with your work. Your baby will be happiest if the playpen is in the same room as you are, where he can see you and you can talk to him. Playpens are also useful for out-of-doors.

There are two main styles of playpen. The traditional, long-lasting wooden type is made with vertical, parallel bars. This sort is best with a built-in floor, to prevent it from being shunted along by your child. For safety, avoid using a playpen with horizontal playbeads. These can be used as 'ladder rungs' by active babies determined to explore. The other sort of playpen is mesh-sided, with a raised, built-in floor. It has a padded rim, and this, together with its soft sides, makes it less likely that your baby would hurt himself if he slipped or fell down inside it. Check that it doesn't have V-shaped legs in which an older child outside could trap his head or limbs.

BABY CARRIERS

With a baby carrier or sling, you can carry your baby around, both indoors and out, held safely and securely against your body. As well as being soothing for your baby, it leaves your hands free for other tasks.

When choosing a carrier, make sure that you can put it on and take it off without needing help. Washable fabrics are practical and a removable head support allows the carrier to be used with new babies as well as older ones. Older babies can also be carried in the baby carrier on your back.

For a baby old enough to support his own head and sit up by himself, you can use a kiddy carrier – a sort of sit-in backpack. Make sure that it has attachment points for a safety harness and look for one with a free-standing frame, so you can clip your child into it and then put it on by yourself.

BUYING TOYS

It is not necessary for you to spend a lot of money providing a cupboard full of toys for your baby. It is far more important to have a few well-chosen items that are appropriate for his age and stage of development. Outsize teddies and animals, for example, may look fun, but babies prefer a variety of smaller things – they are far easier to hold, cuddle, explore and chew! Larger toys are best kept for when they are older.

As well as entertaining your baby, toys help him learn about shape, colour, texture and sound, and about how he can affect his surroundings. It's a big step the day your baby learns that if he moves his hand, the rattle he is holding makes a noise. Later on, he will enjoy toys that need more dexterity: he will be able to squeeze squeaky toys, roll a ball, turn the pages of a board book and even build a small tower of fabric bricks.

TOYS FOR YOUR YOUNG BABY:

▶ rattles
▶ pram beads
▶ mirror (only use one specially made for babies)
▶ activity centre
▶ small soft toys
▶ mobiles (hung out of reach)
▶ small picture books

TOYS FOR YOUR OLDER BABY:

▶ ball
▶ play telephone
▶ push-along toys
▶ squeaking toys
▶ bath toys
▶ shape-sorter toys

SAFETY

▶ Never give your baby anything small enough to swallow or anything which might break or shatter when handled or bitten.
▶ Check that eyes, buttons and ribbons on toys are secure (tie-on ribbons should be removed from toys intended for babies).
▶ Never put your baby in a bouncer until he can hold up his head without support.

▶ Never leave your baby unattended in his bouncer, and always supervise him very closely especially if you have other children or animals about.
▶ Make sure the doorway is kept clear and there is no danger of the door suddenly slamming shut.
▶ If you're buying a second-hand bouncer, or borrowing one, check the suspension strap for wear.

▶ *See page 35 for bath toys*

ACTIVITY EQUIPMENT

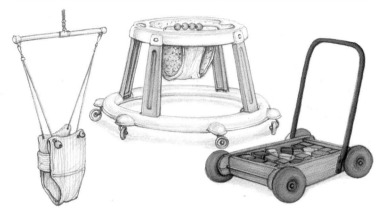

Most babies get a lot of enjoyment from activity equipment, as well as from toys they can hold. You may like to think about buying a baby bouncer, once your baby can support his own head (from about three months onwards). This is a fabric saddle, suspended on a frame clamped to a doorway. Your baby is placed in the saddle and can gently bounce in an upright position. It's a great way to keep your baby entertained – though don't leave him in the bouncer for too long. After a short while, he'll want to be taken out for a change of position and scene.

Later on, when your baby is able to sit up, he may enjoy using a baby walker to get around. This is a small seat, in a lightweight frame of plastic or metal, on castors. Your baby can propel himself by 'walking' along the floor. A baby walker won't actually help your child learn to walk any quicker than he would otherwise – and in fact, your baby needs plenty of time on the floor, learning to crawl, pull himself up and to walk unaided – but used properly, it can give your baby an entertaining experience and relieve the frustration of a baby who longs to be upright, but who hasn't quite got there yet! It is quite a bulky item to have and is therefore not really suitable for use in small homes, but if you want one, check that it folds flat for storage.

A baby who is just beginning to walk by himself will get a lot of fun from a wooden push-along toddle truck. Check that the one you choose is sturdy and stable. This sort of toy is played with for a long time after it has been used to give a learner-walker fun and extra confidence. The truck becomes a pretend pram and a storehouse for treasures – and the bricks in it will give years of good play value too.

BABY WALKER SAFETY

A baby walker can be hazardous unless you are careful to supervise your baby while he is using it, so never leave him unattended in it. He must not use his walker anywhere that he might come into contact with household dangers such as hot drinks, wires, fires, ungated stairs or a change of level. Even quite small changes of surface like the edge of a carpet or a carpet rod could cause the walker to tip over. Don't allow an older toddler to either play near the walker when your baby is in it or to use the walker himself.

OUT AND ABOUT

Choosing the right sort of outdoor transport for your baby looks like a difficult task – after all, there are so many options available. It is true that the choice can seem confusing, but in fact it only reflects the wide range of needs that different families have. When considering what to buy for your new baby, remember that it is best for a baby to lie flat for the first few months of life.

It pays to take time in choosing what you need; shop at a store where they allow you ample opportunity to look at and try out what they have on offer. You need to have the chance to push the items you like the look of; check that the handle is a comfortable height for you and, if it is a folding model, have a go at folding it and see how easy – or difficult – it feels. Try lifting it to make sure that it is light enough for you to carry without straining yourself. Take your partner along, so he can try the equipment out as well. It is important that he also feels comfortable with anything you buy.

You may be able to get one single item that will suit your baby and your lifestyle from birth to toddlerhood. More likely, you will end up with two or more – though before doing this, take a close look at the new and versatile three-in-one transport systems that change and grow with your baby.

WHAT TO CHOOSE

You will need to think about the sort of use your transport will be put to and the amount of space you have in which to store it. Are you likely to be driving to the shops or to visit friends with it? Are you short of space to accommodate it at home? Do you have steps up or down to your house or flat? If so, then think about getting a carrycot/traveller that comes with its own detachable transporter. You may then decide that an easy-to-fold stroller or pushchair will be useful when your baby is a little older. On the other hand, if you have the space at home and plan on doing your shopping nearby, a pram may suit you better to begin with.

PRAMS, TRAVELLERS AND CARRYCOTS

Hard-bodied prams will give years of hard wear and will certainly last through two, three or more children. You can usually get a good deal of shopping below the body if you have a shopping tray. A baby in a pram is well protected from the coldest of weathers and, because the pram tends to be fairly high up, with your baby facing you, you can have a good 'conversation' with her when she is sitting up. Many people like the traditional appeal of a 'proper pram' and many new models now incorporate a detachable, collapsible chassis which makes them easier to store than they once were.

On the other hand, they are generally more expensive than soft-bodied prams, or carrycots/travellers and transporters, and not as nippy to push round town as strollers and pushchairs. Bear in mind if you live in a flat above ground level without a lift, or have steps up or down from your front door, you may find a pram rather awkward to manoeuvre. A compromise that means less cost, greater adaptability but a shorter useful life is to choose a traveller (pram-type top) or a carrycot, plus a separate chassis or transporter (wheels). It is easy to separate the top from the wheels, which makes storage less of a problem and means that it can be used, with a safety restraint, to carry a baby in the back seat of a car. Don't forget to check that the folded wheels will fit easily into the boot of your car. Carrycots are likely to be smaller and less hardwearing than travellers which have most, if not all, of the space and sturdiness you get with a pram.

STROLLERS AND PUSHCHAIRS

Strollers and pushchairs are useful from when your baby is a few months old. Some models have a reclining position that allows your baby to sleep more comfortably and some pushchairs can be adapted so that the baby can face either towards or away from you. They are deservedly popular, as they are easy to get on and off buses, tubes and trains, and fold for storage when not in use. They are reasonably easy to get through shop doorways, so you can take your baby almost anywhere, and with care even lift her up and over the odd hazard like a short flight of steps. The cost is low, compared to a top-quality pram or traveller and chassis. They do not last for ever, though, and if you have used your stroller or pushchair especially heavily, you may find that it will not last through another child. This is the area of baby transport where the most innovative styling can be found, however, and if you like your baby transport to be design-conscious, with up-to-date 'engineering' to improve performance, then this may be the choice for you.

THREE-IN-ONE SYSTEMS

Three-in-one systems have most of the benefits of a carrycot plus transporter and a pushchair rolled into one. You start off with the carrycot which you can put on wheels to make a pram and then when your baby gets too big for this, or when you need to use public transport or the car, you swap the carrycot for a pushchair seat. You get good looks with this system, too, as there are continual improvements in its adaptability and design. What you may not get is the size of a traveller or a pram, or the lightness of some strollers. And if you have another baby before the first has outgrown the pushchair seat, you will need the wheels once more for the carrycot top. However, they do represent good value for money.

CHOOSING WHAT IS RIGHT FOR YOU

Read our at-a-glance guide to the different options available before
you choose your baby's transport. Whatever you decide is right for
you, check that it has a braking system that operates on two wheels,
not just one, and test the brakes in the shop before you buy. When
buying a pram, traveller or carrycot, check that anchorage points for
a safety harness are fixed to the sides or base and that you are happy
with the security of the brakes on the chassis or transporter. For a
pushchair or stroller, check that there are anchorage points for a
safety harness or that the seat includes its own integral five-point
harness. If it comes with an integral three-point harness, you should
still use a separate safety harness with it. Make sure that any folding
pushchair or stroller is fitted with a primary and secondary locking
device to prevent it accidentally folding up when a child is in it.

PRAM

A pram gives a comfortable ride, with
plenty of room for your baby to lie flat
or sit comfortably until well into her
second or third year. It gives good
protection against the weather all
year round.

Essential extras:
safety harness (for older baby).

Points to look for:
mattress included; detachable,
foldable chassis, with removable
wheels; integral backrest for older
baby.

Useful extras:
shopping tray; insect net; sun
canopy.

SAFETY

▶ Get in the habit of *always* putting
a safety harness on your baby. She
is less likely to object if she learns
to accept the harness as a normal
part of sitting in her pushchair or
pram as well as in her highchair. It
will help you to do this if you keep a
separate harness with each item.

TRAVELLER

A traveller, or pram-type top, is similar to a carrycot, as it separates from its chassis and can be used to carry a baby on the back seat of a car (always use a carrycot restraint for safety, see page 56).

Essential extras:
safety harness (for older baby).

Points to look for:
traveller body folds flat for storage; mattress included; easy-to-fold chassis with detachable wheels; comfortable carrying handles.

Useful extras:
shopping tray; insect net; sun canopy.

CARRYCOT

A carrycot is used while your baby is small, as it is smaller and more lightweight than a traveller or a pram. You can buy a transporter to use with it (see also three-in-one systems, page 53).

Essential extras:
safety harness (for older baby).

Points to look for:
carrycot body folds flat for storage; mattress included; light to carry; comfortable carrying handles.

Useful extras:
transporter; shopping tray for transporter; insect net; sun canopy; carrycot stand for indoors.

PUSHCHAIR

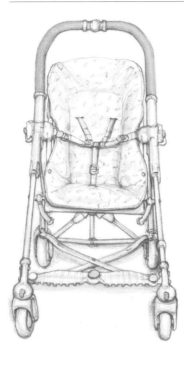

A pushchair that can be adjusted to lie back is suitable for a baby of a few months old and can be useful if you are short of space, or as an extra to a pram or traveller. It can, of course, also be used for older babies and toddlers and should give several years' sturdy service. Most pushchairs fold flat for storage and will fit easily into a car boot.

Points to look for:
reversible/multi-position seat so baby can face away from or towards you, and lie back or sit up; removable seat for easy cleaning; cushioned tyres; reflective wheel discs; folds up with shopping tray in place.

Essential extras:
safety harness (if no integral five-point harness); hood and apron.

Useful extras:
shopping tray (if available on model); sun canopy or parasol; comfort cushion; cosytoes cover.

STROLLER

A stroller is lightweight and easy to handle. It folds up compactly like an umbrella, so you can easily carry it with one hand, making it ideal for use around town or when travelling. If your baby is not yet able to sit up unsupported, choose a style that also has a reclining position. Most strollers have a reinforced seat and an angled back to give extra support to your baby. Look for a model with cushioned tyres to give a smoother, more comfortable ride.

Points to look for:
easy-to-clean seat fabric; easy-folding mechanism; cushioned tyres; reflective wheel discs.

Essential extras:
safety harness (if no integral five-point harness); hood and apron.

Useful extras:
sun canopy or parasol; comfort cushion; cosytoes cover.

THREE-IN-ONE SYSTEM

A 'three-in-one' gives you a transporter, plus a carrycot, plus a pushchair seat. After the baby is a few months old, you can swap the pushchair seat for the carrycot, using the same transporter, whenever you want to. The pushchair can take several positions, including a horizontal one. It can also face towards or away from you.

Essential extras:
safety harness (if no integral five-point harness); hood and apron.

Points to look for:
carrycot body folds flat for storage; mattress included; easy-to-clean seat fabric; easy-folding mechanism; cushioned tyres; reflective wheel discs – check also the ease with which the carrycot and the pushchair fit on to the transporter, and the versatility of the pushchair positions.

Useful extras:
shopping tray (if not included); sun canopy or parasol; comfort cushion; cosytoes cover; insect net.

TRANSPORT FOR TWO

If you have twins, or two children very close in age, then you have special demands to make of your transport!

TWIN PRAMS

Your babies lie (and later sit) at either end of a twin pram, which is normally slightly longer and wider than a standard-size pram with two hoods.

Essential extras:
two safety harnesses.

Points to look for:
mattress included; detachable, foldable chassis with removable wheels.

Useful extras:
shopping tray; parasol/canopy (not always available for twin prams).

TWIN PUSHCHAIRS AND STROLLERS

If the twin pushchair or stroller has seats that can be adjusted to lie back, it can be used with babies of a few months old. An option available with some models is to replace one or both of the seats with a carrycot (obviously, it has to be the carrycot made to go with this particular model). This gives an ideal form of transport for a new baby and an older brother or sister as well as for twins.

Points to look for:
easy-to-clean seat fabric; easy-folding mechanism; reflective wheel discs; independently adjustable positions for seat backs.

Essential extras:
two safety harnesses; hood and apron.

Useful extras:
parasols/canopies; comfort cushions; cosytoes covers.

THE SAFETY HARNESS

This is an absolute must, for use in prams, carrycots, travellers and in pushchairs and strollers without their own integral five-point harness. You should always use a harness with a highchair, as well. Slip the separate anchor straps through the anchorage points in the pram (or wherever you are using the harness) and attach the harness to the straps. When your baby starts to walk, you can use the walking rein with the same harness.

HOOD AND APRON

To give all-weather protection to your baby in her pushchair or stroller, you'll need a transparent, ventilated hood and apron. This fits over the frame and allows your baby an unrestricted view while keeping her out of the wind and rain.

EXTRA EXTRA...

You may decide that you don't need all of these 'useful extras' – but they may make life easier for you and journeys more comfortable for your baby.

▶ A shopping tray is very helpful and stops you draping shopping from the handles of your pram or pushchair (which can tip it up). Check that the one you buy fits properly – chassis and transporters with a central brake will need a different sort of tray, for instance, and some pushchair/stroller transporters cannot take a slide-under tray because of their framework.

▶ A comfort cushion is especially useful for smaller babies, who may be uncomfortable at first in a pushchair or stroller, though it gives extra comfort to babies and toddlers of all ages. It helps to keep your pushchair/stroller seat clean, too.

▶ A cosytoes cover is a much more convenient and efficient way to keep your baby warm than blankets and covers, which have a habit of trailing on the ground. Some are available in smart colourways to tone with your push-chair. Choose either a box style or a two-legged style. If your pushchair has an integral harness, check that the cover has holes through which the straps can be threaded.

▶ Parasols or canopies are especially useful in summer weather and essential, in fact, if you take your pushchair or stroller abroad to a hot country. You can buy a clip-on parasol or a hinged parasol, both of which can be angled to keep your baby in the shade.

▶ A hooded raincover which fits round your baby and her pushchair/stroller is no substi-tute for the essential hood and apron but it can be used for showery weather. Keep one in the bottom of your bag for emergency use.

SAFETY IN THE CAR

It is vital to make sure that your baby is as secure as possible when she is a car passenger — right from the start. The good news is that this is now easier to do than ever before. Products available today are simple to use and well designed to keep your baby secure and comfortable. There is a considerable choice of different options for your new baby and for your older child.

FOR YOUR NEW BABY

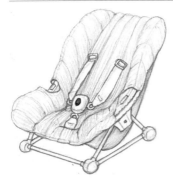

▶ A rearward-facing car seat, specially designed for babies from birth up to 10 kilograms (22lb) or about nine months in age. To secure this type of seat, you use one of your car's existing adult seat belts, either in the front or the back of the car, and your baby is held in the seat by an adjustable shoulder and crotch harness. It is useful if the seat is free-standing and if it has integral carrying handles.

▶ A rearward-facing, two-stage car seat that changes into a forward-facing car seat for your older baby. Used in the rearward-facing position, it is suitable for babies up to 10 kilograms (22lb) in weight or about nine months in age. It secures with an existing lap and diagonal seat belt in the front or back seat of the car.

▶ A carrycot/traveller restraint, which fixes to the car with a suitable four-point anchorage kit. This allows your baby's carrycot to lie on the back seat of your car, securely restrained in the event of a collision or sudden braking or swerving. Be sure to put a safety harness on your baby, attaching it to the anchorage points, and clip on the apron of the carrycot when she is in it.

Carrycot restraints are considerably cheaper than car seats, but you need to bear in mind that the carrycot takes up most of the room in the back seat. A baby car seat is very versatile, as it can be taken from car to car without any problem, simply using the existing front or rear seat belts. This makes it especially useful when you are in a car that is not your own.

FOR YOUR OLDER CHILD

The choice for your older child is between the forward-facing position of the two-stage car seat and a car seat designed for a baby from 9 kilograms (20lb). If you already have a two-stage car seat, you can use this for your older baby in the forward-facing position and on the back seat of the car where it can be fixed with an adult seat belt or suitable anchorage kit. In this position it is suitable for a child from 9 kilograms (20lb) up to about 18 kilograms (40lb) or about four years in age. If you are buying a car seat designed for an older baby you can choose between those that are fixed with adult seat belts and those that fix to an anchorage kit; some models also recline to allow her to sleep more comfortably. A play and feeding tray is available for some car seats and can be useful on a long journey.

Make it a rule that you never drive with your child unless she is secured in her car seat. This is especially important once she can undo the restraint. Always stop the car and refasten the harness.

SEAT BELTS AND ANCHORAGE KITS

You can fit your own seat belts in most cars, using the pre-drilled holes on the chassis. If you follow the instructions carefully, it is not a difficult job to do yourself, though of course you can get it done at a garage. If your car was made before 1981, it may not have pre-drilled points, in which case you will need to ask a garage to drill them for you. Once installed, rear seat belts can also be used with a booster seat when your child outgrows her car seat.

Similarly, fixing an anchorage kit for use with a carrycot restraint or car seat is not difficult and the kit can be used with a junior car harness when your child is larger. You will need to buy the appropriate kit, according to whether your car is a hatchback/estate or a saloon model.

Using an anchorage kit designed for a hatchback or estate does mean that your luggage space becomes restricted because of the long straps needed to secure the car seat or carrycot restraint. To solve this problem, think about installing a special 'space saver' bar which you use with a saloon anchorage kit. It is simple to install and removes easily when you need to fold the car's rear seat.

IMPORTANT

Children should always be properly restrained when travelling in cars. Babies need *either* a rear-facing car seat, properly secured, *or* to be in a carrycot on the back seat, secured with a special anchorage kit. Older babies need a special car seat, secured either by its own anchorage kit or with an existing rear seat belt, as appropriate. Older children should wear a junior car harness or use an adult lap and diagonal rear seat belt with a booster seat.

If you have an accident in your car, or even if you have to brake suddenly or swerve to avoid an accident, your baby is in great danger. If unrestrained, she can be thrown against the hard surfaces of the car, or even thrown through the windscreen, with tremendous and possibly fatal force. Drivers, even when they themselves are properly restrained in a seat belt, are sometimes severely or fatally injured by an unrestrained baby or child being thrown against them.

SAFETY AROUND THE HOUSE

It is never too soon to start thinking about safety. Of course, when your baby is small you won't need to have your house equipped with baby gates and cooker guards, but even a tiny baby can begin to roll sooner than you realize. Take appropriate measures to minimize risks and hazards well before your baby reaches the stage when he can crawl, walk or climb into trouble.

FROM BIRTH

▶ Check stairs for loose carpet.
▶ Secure trailing flexes with cable clips.
▶ Check baby equipment for safety, especially if bought second-hand.
▶ Install a baby alarm.
▶ Make sure heating of baby's room is adequate and safe (see page 37).
▶ Install safe low lighting in baby's room (see page 37).
▶ Make sure the baby bath has a slip-resistant surface or use a slip-resistant baby bathmat in it.

WHEN HE CAN ROLL OVER

▶ Install guards round fires in all rooms where your baby is likely to be.
▶ Use a slip-resistant bathmat when your baby moves into the big bath.
▶ Cover all electrical sockets with special plastic covers.

WHEN HE BEGINS TO CRAWL

▶ Fix baby gate to stairs.
▶ Fix cupboard, drawer and fridge/freezer catches.
▶ Fix window catches.
▶ Fix automatic doorstops.
▶ Fix cooker/hob guard.
▶ Replace leads on kettles and other kitchen equipment with safer, curly ones.
▶ Put corner protectors on furniture.

WHEN HE STARTS TO WALK AND CLIMB

▶ Install safety glass or put safety film on items such as glass doors, French windows, table tops and shower screens.
▶ Fix bookshelves securely to walls and make sure any free-standing pieces of furniture are stable enough not to tip over if a baby pulls himself up on them.

▶ *See pages 60–61 for safety equipment*

GENERAL SAFETY MEASURES

In addition to the safety equipment described on the next page, there are a few safety items that are of general importance in the home.

An automatic smoke detector emits a powerful alarm when it senses smoke, giving vital warning in the event of a fire. It generally runs off a battery and can be fixed by simply screwing it into position on the wall or ceiling.

A fire blanket kept in an easily accessible place – preferably on a wall in the kitchen – is very useful for smothering flames if a pan or a child's clothing catches fire.

Safe lighting: As well as arranging low lighting in your baby's room, think about using it in hallways and other dark areas. A glow light that simply fixes straight into a socket gives a soft, safe light at floor level and may be helpful when you need to get up to attend to your baby. Later on, toddlers and older children find the gentle glow helps them to see their way to the bathroom at night. You can now buy a plug light that automatically switches on as night falls and off as day breaks.

IMPORTANT

Always make sure that you or anyone else looking after your young baby:
▶ never leaves him on his own on a raised surface, even when tiny
▶ always secures him with a safety harness when he is in his highchair, pram or pushchair
▶ never puts your baby in his baby seat on a raised surface
▶ always comes downstairs with one hand holding on to the banister when carrying him
▶ keeps hot drinks, like tea or coffee, well out of his way
▶ always keeps sharp tools and other dangerous items, like household cleaners, locked up and out of a baby's or toddler's reach and puts them away after use
▶ keeps all medicines and tablets in a cupboard out of his reach
▶ keeps polythene wrappings away from both babies and children.

SAFETY EQUIPMENT

A baby alarm links you with your baby when you are in different rooms. It can be used later on, too, if your child is ill and has to stay in bed. Do make sure that you place the 'baby end' of the alarm where your baby cannot reach it.

You can choose a battery-operated alarm, its two 'halves' linked by a thin flex. Make sure the flex doesn't trail. The alternative is the more expensive, but more versatile electronic alarm. The units simply plug into a socket, which means you can very easily move the units from room to room.

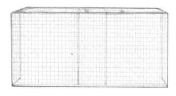

A fireguard is an absolute essential for all fires – electric, gas or open. The only really safe kind extends to cover the whole fireplace. With an open fire, choose a guard that can be fixed securely to the wall and use a spark guard as well.

Plastic socket covers cost very little, yet they are a very effective way to stop little fingers prying and poking into socket holes. Place them over sockets that are not in use – they are easy to remove for an adult, though virtually impossible for a baby or toddler.

A baby gate at the top and/or bottom of the stairs saves a lot of anxiety, as your baby can play in the hall or on the landing without you worrying about tumbles downstairs. You can also use one in open doorways.

A gate with a locking catch is one option – you fix the hinged side to the wall and the catch to the opposite wall. The one shown is adjustable to fit different-sized openings. Alternatively, you can use a removable gate that fits into special wall fixings for the four 'corners' of the gate. Additional fixing kits can be bought so you can easily move the gate to a variety of places – put one set at the top of the stairs and one at the bottom, for example. You can also buy a gate that allows an adult to walk through the middle section.

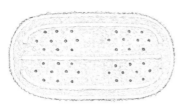

A slip-resistant bathmat for the baby bath or big bath helps prevent your baby from slipping and sliding. It fixes with suction cups and removes easily for bath cleaning. You should still restrain a young baby with your hand, in case he topples over.

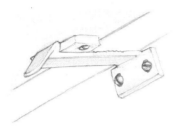

Cupboard and drawer catches are cheap, and quick and easy to fix, and mean that you can shut sharp, breakable (or edible!) items safely out of your baby's way. You can also buy a fridge/freezer catch that has a double action: while restricting inquisitive children from opening it, it still allows you to use the fridge or freezer normally when they are not about.

Window catches for casement windows allow a window to be open for ventilation, but prevents it being opened any wider – good for a child's room.

An automatic doorstop prevents a door slamming on your baby's fingers. It allows you to close the door normally with a gentle push, but stops it closing suddenly.

A cooker or hob guard fits securely round the working edge, and though it allows you to cook normally, it prevents your toddler pulling over pots and pans, providing that you always turn pan handles inwards.

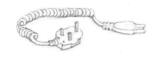

Curly leads for kettles and other kitchen appliances are far safer than normal ones – for everyone in the family, not just your baby or toddler.

Corner protectors on table points, or anywhere else where there are sharp corners, are easy to put on and really do save a lot of tears from bumped heads.

Safety film on glass surfaces inside your home means that glass may shatter under impact, but the broken glass remains in place – so in the event of an accident, no one will be cut by jagged points of glass. Applied properly, the film is smooth and unobtrusive.

USEFUL ADDRESSES

When writing to any of these organizations for information, please enclose a stamped addressed envelope.

Association of Breastfeeding Mothers
131 Mayow Road
London SE26 4HZ
(01) 778 4769
Provides information, leaflets and counselling. Contact for a list of your local counsellors.

British Standards Institute
2 Park Street
London W1A 2BS
(01) 629 9000
Publishes leaflets on standards for safe toys and equipment for babies and young children.

CRY-SIS
BM CRY-SIS
London WC1N 3XX
(01) 404 5011
Offers support, information and counselling for parents of babies who cry excessively.

Gingerbread
35 Wellington Street
London WC2E 7BN
(01) 240 0953
Provides information, friendship and social support for single parents. Local branches nationwide.

La Leche League
BM 3424
London WC1N 3XX
(01) 242 1278
Runs breastfeeding groups and offers information and counselling. Leaflets available.

The Maternity Alliance
15 Britannia Street
London WC1X 9JP
(01) 837 1265
Gives information on benefits and employment rights for all pregnant women and mothers.

National Childbirth Trust (NCT)
Alexandra House
Oldham Terrace
London W3 6NH
(01) 992 8637
Runs antenatal classes and offers breastfeeding counselling and postnatal support. Leaflets available. For local branches, see phone book.

One-parent Families
255 Kentish Town Road
London NW5 2LX
(01) 267 1361
Provides information, especially on benefits, housing, legal problems and childcare.

Twins and Multiple Births Association (TAMBA)
The National Secretary
41 Fortuna Way
Aylesby Park
Grimsby
South Humberside
DN37 9SJ
For parents of twins, triplets and other multiple births. Organizes twins clubs nationwide.

Working Mothers Association
23 Webbs Road
London SW11 6RU
(01) 228 3757
Gives information and support. Leaflets available. Local branches nationwide.

INDEX

A

Alarms, baby 36, 60
Amusing babies 43
Anchorage kits, car 57
Anoraks 13
Aprons, pushchair 55

B

Bathing babies 30–1
  dislike of big bath 35
  equipment 32, 33
  newborn babies 34
  older babies 35
  and safety 33
  toys 35
Bathmats, slip-resistant
  61
Beakers, trainer 19
Bibs 11, 20
  and safety 19
Blanket boxes 37
Bodysuits 8
Bonnets 9
Bootees 8, 13
Bottlefeeding 14
  choosing bottles and
    teats 16, 19
  making up feeds 18
  safety tips 19
  sterilizing equipment
    17
Bottle warmers 16
Bouncers, baby 47
  and safety 46
Bouncing cradles 44
Bowls, baby 20
Bras, nursing 15
Breastfeeding 14
  for comfort 43
  equipment 15
Briefs, fabric 11
Buckets, nappy 25
Bumpers, cot 40
  and safety 41

C

Canopies 55
Cardigans 9, 12
Carriers, baby 45
  and safety 44
Carrycots 51
  bedding 38, 42
  car restraints for 56
  clothing for 11, 13, 42
  as first bed 38
Carrycot/travellers 48

Car seats 56, 57
Chairs, rocking 44
Changing bags 27
Changing mats 28
Climbing babies 58
Clothes:
  0–3 months 6–9, 11
  3–4 months 12
  for crawling babies
    13
  for night-time 12
  for outdoors 13
  and safety 9, 11
  washing 6, 8
Comfort blankets 41
Convector heaters 37
Cooker guards 61
Corner protectors 61
Cosytoes covers 55
Cot beds 39
Cots 39
  bedding 40
  mattresses 40
  and safety 38
  second-hand 39
  toys for 40
Cradles 38
Crawling babies:
  clothes 13
  and safety 58
Cream, baby 27
Cribs 38
Crying, coping with 43
Cupboard catches 61
Cups, first 19
Cushions, comfort 55
Cutlery, babies' 20

D

Decorating babies'
  rooms 37
Dimmer switches 37
Disposable nappies 22,
  23, 26
  disposing of 26
  putting on 29
  and safety 26
Doorstops, automatic
  61
Drawer catches 61
Dressers, baby 28, 37
Dressing babies 10
  easy clothes for 7
Duvets, cot 40

F

Fabrics, choosing 6

Feeding babies see
  Bottlefeeding;
  Breastfeeding;
  Foods, commercial;
  Weaning
Fire blankets 59
Fireguards 60
Fires 37
Flexes 61
Flooring 37
Foods, commercial 20
Formula milk see
  Bottlefeeding
Freezer catches 61
Friezes 37
Furnishing babies'
  rooms 37

G

Gates, safety 60
Glass, safety film for 61
Glow lights 37, 59
Gowns, baby 11
'Grow-tall' steps 29

H

Harnesses, safety 55
Hats 9, 13
Heating 36, 37
Highchairs:
  choosing 21
  safety points 21
Hob guards 61
Hoods, pushchair 55
Hot weather, clothes for
  11

J

Jogging suits 13
Jugs, measuring 16
Jumpers 9, 12

K

Kettles, leads for 61
Knitted items 8, 9

L

Lamps 37
  and safety 37
Lavatory training seats
  29

Leads, curly 61
Lighting 37
    and safety 59
Lotion, baby 27

M

Matinée jackets 9
Mattresses, cot 40
    and safety 41
Medicines 59
Microwave ovens: and
    bottlefeeding 19
Mittens 8
    scratch 11
Mobiles, cot 40
    and safety 41
Moses baskets 38
    and safety 38
Musical toys 40

N

Nappies:
    changing 27, 28, 29
    disposable 22, 23, 26
    terry 22, 23, 24, 25
    washing 25
Nappy liners 24
Nappy pins 24
Nappy rash 26, 27
Nightlights 37, 59
Nightwear 12

O

Outdoors, going 42
    clothes for 13

P

Pants, waterproof 24
Parasols 13, 55
Pelican bibs 20
Pillows 38
Plates, baby 20
Playpens 45
    playmats for 44
Playsuits 9, 13
Potty chairs 29
Potty training 29
Prams 48, 49, 50
    bedding 42
    clothes for 11, 13, 42
    extras for 50, 55
    and safety 50
    for twins 54

Pram suit 11
Pushchairs 48, 49, 52
    extras for 52, 55
    for twins 54
Pyjamas 12

R

Raincovers, pushchair
    55
Rash, nappy 26, 27
Refrigerator catches 61
Rockers, baby 44

S

Safety:
    in babies' rooms 37
    at bathtime 33
    and bottlefeeding 19
    in cars 56–7
    and chairs and
        carriers 44
    and clothes 9, 11
    and cots 38, 39
    around the house
        58–9
    with toys 41, 46
Scratch mittens 11
Seat belts, car 57
Shawls 8, 9
Shopping trays 55
Sizing clothes 7
Sleepers, walk-in 12
Sleeping:
    in the day, 36, 42
    at night 36, 41
Sleeping bags 11
Slings, baby 45
Smoke detectors 59
Snowsuits 13
Socket covers 60
Solid food see Weaning
Spoons, baby 20
Stairs: and safety 58,
    59
Sterilizing bottlefeeding
    equipment 17
Stretchsuits 7, 8, 9, 12
Strollers 48, 49, 52
    extras for 52, 55
    for twins 54
Sun hats 9, 13

T

Table-and-lowchair unit
    21

Tables, corner
    protectors for 61
Table seats,
    foldaway 21
Teats, choosing 16, 19
Tee-shirts 11
Terry nappies 22, 23,
    24
    changing 27, 28, 29
    folding 25
    washing 25
'Three-in-one' systems
    49, 53
    extras for 53
Toddle trucks 47
Topping and tailing 31
Toys 43, 46
    for cots 40
    and safety 41, 46
    storing 37
Trainer beakers 19
Transporters, carrycot
    48, 49, 51, 53
Travel cots 41
Travellers 48, 49, 51
    extras for 51, 55
Twins:
    prams for 54
    pushchairs and
        strollers for 54

V

Vests 8, 11, 12

W

Walkers, baby 47
    and safety 47
Walking: and safety 58
Wallpaper 37
Washing babies see
    Bathing; Topping
    and tailing
Washing clothes 6, 8
Waterproof pants 24
    washing 25
Weaning 15
    equipment 20
Window catches 61
Wipes, baby 27

Z

Zinc and castor oil
    cream 27